Horse Trams of the British Isles

by
R.W. Rush

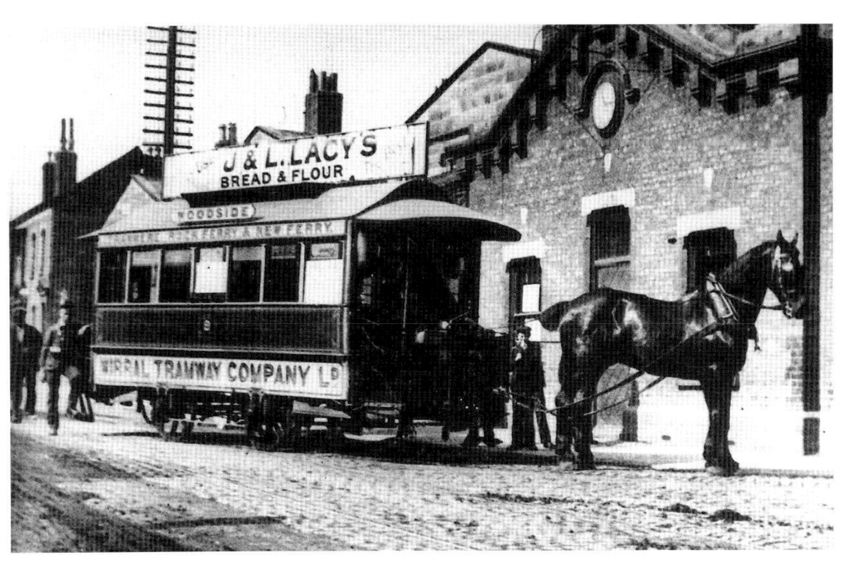

THE OAKWOOD PRESS

British Library Cataloguing in Publication Data
A Record for this book is available from the British Library
ISBN 0 85361 600 0

Typeset by Oakwood Graphics.
Repro by Ford Graphics, Ringwood, Hants.
Printed by Cambrian Printers Ltd, Aberystwyth, Ceredigion.

Title page: The Wirral Tramway Co. Ltd was one of three different companies all running horse tramways in Birkenhead in the early days. It completed its three mile route from Woodside Ferry (for Liverpool) straight down the main Chester Road to the New Ferry toll bar at Bebington Road, on 19th January, 1878. The tramway was purchased in 1895 by Birkenhead Corporation but leased back to the company until closure in May 1900 for electrification. Because of a low railway bridge at Tranmere only single-deck cars could be used, of which there were seven small ones at first, built locally by Starbuck. In 1879 they were replaced by seven larger Starbuck single-deck cars, plus two more in 1880. Four double-deckers were bought in 1894-1896, probably built by Milnes, but because of the bridge they could not work the full length of the route. Our picture shows turtle-back roof car No. 9, built by Starbuck in 1880, standing outside the depot at the New Ferry terminus in about 1898.
H.G. Dibdin

Front cover: This car is a replica of Bradford Tramways Omnibus Co. Car No. 40 built by WGH Transportation Engineering of Old Edlington, Yorkshire in 1992. It is seen here at Bradford Industrial Museum on 21st August, 1996. The original No. 40 was acquired by Bradford's Tramways & Omnibus Co. in 1892. It would have been used on the route from Rawson Square to Victor Road.
R.P. Barnes

Rear cover: Douglas Corporation's No. 18 on the Promenade at Douglas on 22nd August, 1995. This double-deck vehicle has an interesting history. It was purchased from South Shields Tramways & Carriage Co. Ltd in 1887, in the winter of 1903/04 it was converted to a single deck 'Winter Saloon'. No. 18 saw use along the Douglas Promenade in the winter months until 1926/27, when the winter service ceased to operate. From then onwards No. 18 saw use in poor weather during the summer months. In the winter of 1988/89 this car was rebuilt once again, into the double-deck form shown in this view.
P.G. Barnes

Published by The Oakwood Press (Usk), P.O. Box 13, Usk, Mon., NP15 1YS.
E-mail: sales@oakwoodpress.co.uk
Website: www.oakwoodpress.co.uk

Contents

For the centenary of the Douglas horse tramway in 1976 open toast rack car No. 12 was restored to 1934 condition with lamps mounted on arches at either end. The car was built by G.F. Milnes in 1888 to the original 1884 Starbuck design. *P.H. Abell*

The City of Gloucester Tramways Co. Ltd's Bristol Road cross-city route from Wotton was extended at the late date (by horse standards) of 10th July, 1897 from Theresa Place to Tuffley Avenue. Here we see car No. 13 standing at the new terminus. It is a 24-seat 4-bench summer toast rack car built by the Gloucester Railway Carriage & Wagon Co. Ltd, whose factory was on the same route opposite Theresa Place.

Introduction

The first type of public railed transport, the horse tramway, seems to have been sadly neglected by historians; indeed in published histories of tramway systems all over the country the horse car era has either been omitted, or at best, merely mentioned in passing. Very few detailed accounts have been available. To a large extent, as the author has found during his researches, very little information has been handed down, mainly from the failure of the private companies who operated most of the horse tramways to keep proper records, contenting themselves with the meagre statutory returns which had to be made under the Companies Act.

This is not intended to be a detailed history of all horse tramways, indeed such an attempt would be nigh impossible, and if achieved, would produce a ponderous tome mainly a repetition of local feuds and statistics. It seeks only to trace the development (of which there was not a great deal) from the inception, well over a century ago, of the horse tramways in general, and to compare some of the various designs of cars, and the firms who built them. A list of horse car systems in the British Isles is given as an Appendix, and is believed to be complete as far as the author can discover. There may be slight errors in the statistics - these have been extremely difficult to discover, and have had to rely largely on already-published data, which in some cases are conflicting, and not too reliable. However, the best has been done bearing in mind the paucity of information.

All the drawings of tramcars in this volume have been reproduced to a scale of 4 mm to 1 ft.

Grateful thanks must be expressed to various people who have helped in their various ways, in particular the London Transport Executive for checking the details of the London systems, and to Messrs Ian Cormack, Alan Brotchie, N.N. Forbes, and J.H. Price. Finally, thanks are due to John Gillham who meticulously checked the text and wrote the captions for the photographs.

It is hoped that the book will throw some light on what hitherto has been a very neglected subject.

Robert W. Rush
Accrington

The idea of passenger street tramways originated in Baltimore, USA, with a line opened in about 1828, followed by New Orleans and New York (Harlem) in 1832. John Stephenson, of New York, is reputed to have built the first tramcar in the world, and subsequently built up a huge business supplying trams to many parts of the rest of the world. This picture is said to be the world's first street tramcar. The wording under the entrance step reads 'Stephenson Patent', and along the waistrail reads 'New York-Yorkville-Harlaem'.

The first street horse tramway in Britain was opened in March 1859 by W.J. Curtis at Liverpool, along the line of the docks. This was followed on 30th August, 1860 by the Birkenhead Street Railway Co. Ltd with a 2½ mile route from Woodside Ferry to Birkenhead Park, of which we see here the opening ceremony in Hamilton Square and one of its four cars. The man at the left end of the upper deck with arm outstretched is the genius who built it, the famous George Francis Train, and the boy at the other end of the top deck is the equally famous (in later years) James Clifton Robinson, two of Britain's greatest ever tramway pioneers. *The Birkenhead News*

Chapter One

Historical Background

The horse tram was a natural development from the horse bus, which in turn evolved from the private horse-drawn carriages of innumerable types in which the gentry made their journeys from place to place. For the middle class, there were stage coaches which plied between various towns all over the country, some short distance journeys, but others over lengthy routes, such as London to York or Manchester, which took three or four days. As for the hoi-polloi, they were condemned to travel on foot, or by cadging a lift on carriers' carts, unless they had a little money to spend, in which case they could hire a cab, or as a last resort, a sedan chair. Incidentally, Peterborough is said to have been the last city in this country to have a regular sedan chair service, which lasted until 1864. To make it easier for the ordinary people to get around in the larger towns and cities, there began a service of horse-drawn omnibuses about the middle of the 19th century, in London they proliferated from 1832. From evidence in various publications, in London it was no easier to cross a main thoroughfare in Victorian days than it is today. The streets were jammed with horse-drawn vehicles of all descriptions, which often came to a dead stop, as does modern motor transport at the present time. Taken all round, the average speed of transport in London and other major cities is little faster today than it was a century ago, and, as now, a pedestrian took his life in his hands whenever he tried to cross a main street. So much for 'progress'. Add to the chaos of horse-drawn traffic the filth caused by the excretions of thousands of animals, the dust, in dry weather, thrown up by their passage over the road surfaces of the day, and the resultant mud in wet weather, we can say that in spite of diesel and petrol fumes, pollution these days is far less than that which our Victorian ancestors had to put up with.

Though the Oystermouth Railway (Swansea & Mumbles) operated horse-drawn carriages from 1807, this was not a town tramway and when one gets down to the bottom of the subject, the horse-drawn tramcar, running on fixed rails, was definitely an American invention. By the middle of the century it had become well established in many large and small American towns. By 1850, the system in Philadelphia was one of the largest and most successful. It was here that John G. Brill first began to build horse trams, and laid down the foundations of what was to become the largest tramcar construction company in the world. Though few of Brill's complete cars ever were exported to England (in fact more of Stephenson's products were seen here), the enormous quantity of the company's trucks for electric cars were the mainstay of the British industry almost throughout its existence.

In 1850 a young American named George Francis Train came to Liverpool as the agent of his uncle's shipping company. Young Train became very fond of England, and remained in Liverpool for 10 years, interspersed by journeys abroad in the course of business. In 1858, having returned from a visit to Philadelphia, and being much impressed by the success of the horse tramway

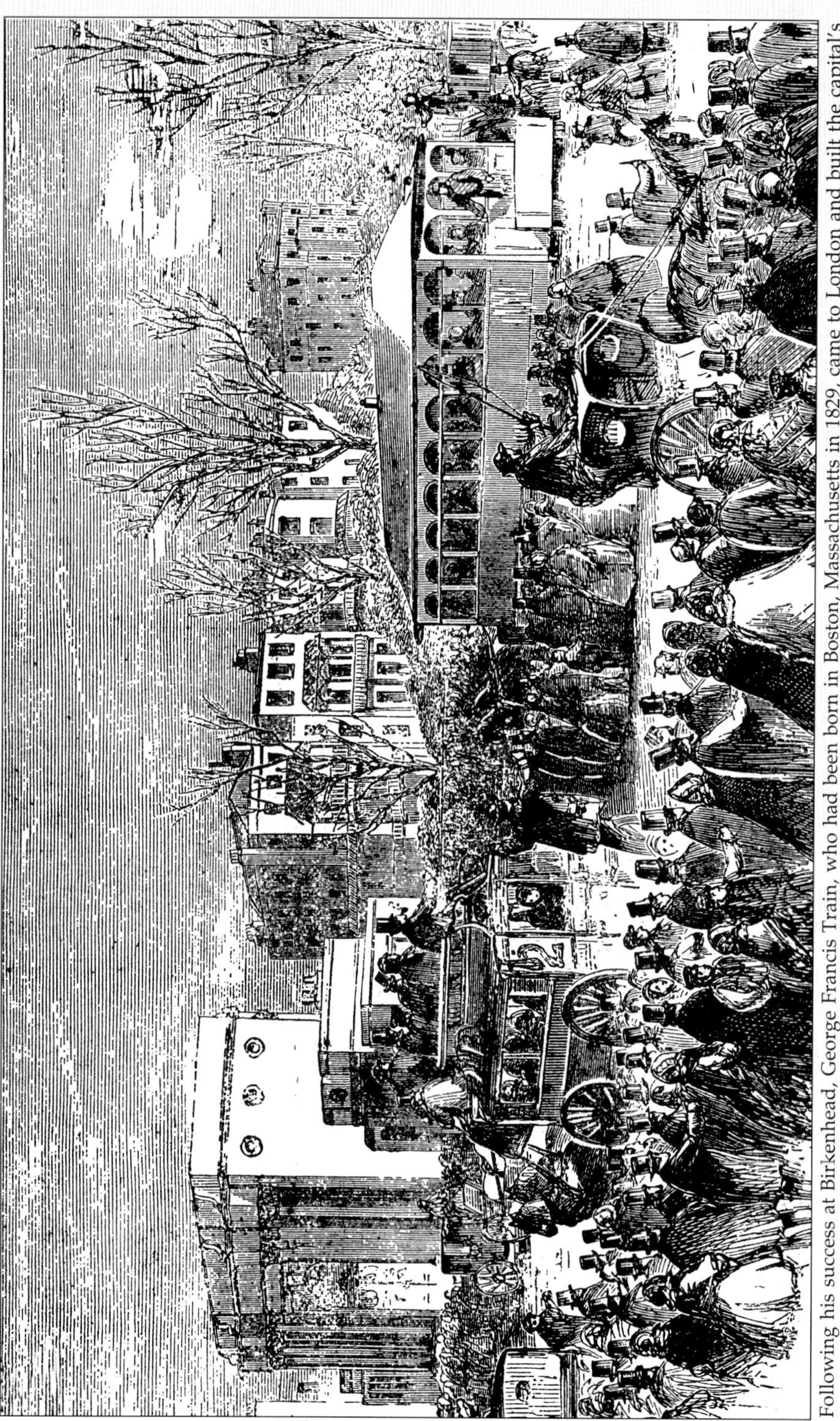

Following his success at Birkenhead, George Francis Train, who had been born in Boston, Massachusetts in 1829, came to London and built the capital's first tramway, the Marble Arch Street Rail Co. Ltd, from Marble Arch along Bayswater Road nearly to Notting Hill Gate. This somewhat over-enthusiastic view shows the opening ceremony on 23rd March, 1861. It was a great success in itself, but was forced to close by mid-September, killed by officialdom and red tape. On the left we see a typical horse omnibus.

system there, he endeavoured to interest the City of Liverpool in a similar project. The Liverpool city fathers, however, would have none of it, but undaunted, Train crossed the river to Birkenhead, where after some considerable argument, he succeeded in obtaining a concession from the local authorities to construct an experimental line along Conway Street to Birkenhead Park, a distance of 1½ miles, forming the Birkenhead Street Railway Company Ltd on 7th May, 1860. The line was opened on 30th August, 1860, and thus became the second public street tramway in the British Isles. (The first was the Line of Docks line at Liverpool by W.J. Curtis in March 1859.) To work the line, Train imported two Stephenson single-deck cars from America, followed shortly afterwards by a pair of double-deck cars. The Birkenhead Street Railway Company Ltd eventually extended the line and relaid the original track, selling out the undertaking to Birkenhead Corporation in 1889. The Corporation in turn leased the system to a newly-formed Birkenhead United Tramways Co. Ltd, who operated for a further 12 years, until in 1901 the Corporation took full possession and converted the lines to electric working.

Encouraged by his experiment, Train transferred his attentions to London. Here he met strenuous opposition, but late in 1860 he did obtain permission to lay an experimental line from Marble Arch which was opened in March 1861, and was known as the Bayswater Tramway. Two were built by Prentiss of Birkenhead to work the line, and these cars bore names - *Princess Royal* and *Her Majesty* - following the practice long established of naming stage coaches. His Victoria Street car was named *The People*, and the first two Darlington cars were *Nelson* and *Wellington*. The naming idea, however, never caught on, apart from a short period in the 1930s, when South Shields Corporation applied names (as well as numbers) to a few of their electric fleet.

Train also succeeded in opening two other short lines in London, in 1861, one from Victoria Station to Parliament Square, and the other from the east end of Westminster Bridge to Kennington Gate. There was sustained and vociferous opposition to all three lines, not only from the local authorities and the London General Omnibus Company, but also from the cab drivers and the well-to-do people of Bayswater. These objections crystallised into one main complaint, the use by Train of the so-called 'step rail' which projected ⅝ in. above the surface of the roadway causing inconvenience to drivers of other vehicles. It soon became apparent that if the light wheels of dog-carts, carriages and cabs were driven across the rails with even reasonable speed, these wheels were often wrenched off their axles, and when the same thing happened to the heavier vehicles of the Omnibus Company, the outcry against the tramways became extreme. As a result, Train was presented with an ultimatum to remove the whole of his apparatus from the streets of London forthwith, and bowing to the inevitable, Train reluctantly complied before the end of 1862. Thereafter, the powers that be in the various parts of the Metropolis steadfastly refused to allow tramways of any kind to be constructed for eight years, when at last there was a change of thinking, and horse tramways began to appear in many parts of the capital. The high and mighty of Bayswater congratulated themselves on having achieved a great victory, and only one of Train's routes ever again became a tramway - that from Westminster Bridge to Kennington Gate.

Only three weeks after the Marble Arch line, Train also opened the Westminster Street Rail Co. Ltd's line from near the north entrance to Westminster Abbey, along Victoria Street as far as the parish boundary almost at Vauxhall Bridge Road. This was on 15th April, 1861, only half a mile long, and worked by only one car, which was built by George Starbuck at Birkenhead, basically similar to the original Stephenson design. Starbuck quickly built up a big business, with many export orders around the world, which later evolved into the famous G.F. Milnes & Co. Ltd of Birkenhead, one of Britain's biggest-ever tramcar builders. The Victoria Street line was again forced to close by officialdom, on 6th March, 1862. Train also built a third tramway, from Westminster Bridge to Kennington Park, which survived only 10 months before meeting the same fate, he then returned to America in 1862, disgusted with English prohibitions on progress with tramways, which by now were flourishing in many different American cities.

Topical Press

Though defeated in his object of bringing tramways to London, Train refused to be discouraged. A remarkable facet of his character was that however great the pressure he was subjected to, and no matter how he was execrated on all sides, his unfailing courtesy and good temper in his dealings with authority was outstanding. Never once did he make an angry outburst, or write an impolite letter. Train transferred his attentions to the Midlands, and obtained permission to construct a line in the Potteries, between Hanley, Burslem, Longton and Fenton, though in actual fact, only the short length between the two first-named towns was built by him. The rails removed from London (and probably the cars too) were used; at all events, the Potteries line started with step-rails, but after two years they were replaced by grooved rails laid flush with the road surface. Train returned to America, disappointed with his fight to bring tramways to Britain, leaving behind only two short lengths, hardly 2½ miles all told, as the result of all his effort. Both of these lines were now in the hands of private companies, both survived and expanded, becoming moderately successful, but the Potteries line was operated by steam traction from 1881.

With the passing of the Tramways Act in 1870 - an iniquitous Act in some ways, since it threw upon the tramway operators certain conditions which were to harass them for years to come - horse tramways did re-appear in London, operated by some 14 different companies. From the early 1870s for a further 20 years new lines were constructed all over London, but all used grooved rails of one type or another which did not project above the road surface, thus obviating to a large extent (but not entirely) the criticisms levelled at Train's step-rails. Trouble was still experienced by the narrow wheels of light private carriages - and later, bicycles - becoming jammed in the grooves (this was to last even into electric days), but the strict conservatism of the intelligentsia at last became resigned to the march of progress. However, it is perhaps significant that the first two of Train's layouts, the Marble Arch, and Victoria lines, never again saw tramways of any kind, while the solitary one laid down in one of the poorer quarters, namely Kennington, became first a horse, and later, electric tramway. By 1st January, 1899 almost all the horse tramways in and around London had become the property of the London County Council, who electrified most of them from 1903 on. The last horse trams in London ran until 1912 on the isolated London United Tramways line from Richmond to Kew, Islington to Lower Holloway until 19th July, 1913, South Hackney to West India Docks on 12th August, 1914 and finally Rotherhithe to Bricklayers Arms on 30th April, 1915.

Another pioneer in the tramway field was John Greenwood, who in 1861 built a line from Pendleton, in the west of the town of Salford, into Manchester. This was a most unusual affair, consisting of a pair of smooth iron plates with a single grooved rail between them. Ordinary horse buses, with the normal smooth iron tyres, were employed, but they were fitted with an extra flanged wheel in front, which ran in the grooved rail, and so (in theory) kept the main wheels on the iron plateway. The system was moderately successful, and operated for about 10 years in this form, then gradually expanded into a normal two-railed tramway, and by amalgamation with several omnibus firms became a part of the Manchester Carriage Company in 1865. There was a saying in Manchester which lasted well into the 20th century, 'as useless as a five-

Here we are at one of the busiest junctions in the inner suburbs of London, the Angel, Islington. We are standing in City Road, looking west, and the North Metropolitan Tramways Co. tramcar, which is on its way from Moorgate to the famous Archway Tavern at Highgate, will turn right at this main crossroads into Islington High Street. The big building in the middle of the picture is the Angel Hotel which gives its name to the road junction. On the extreme left we can just see a tram of the London Street Tramways Co. in Pentonville Road, which terminates here at the Angel before returning to Kings Cross and Kentish Town.

Pamlin Prints

wheeled bus', which perhaps throws some light on what the local populace thought of Greenwood's invention. The Manchester Carriage Co. flourished until 1880, when by another amalgamation it became the Manchester Carriage and Tramways Company, which by 1901 had expanded to a combined fleet of 366 horse trams operating on 78 miles of route in Manchester and Salford, supplemented by the steam-operated Manchester, Bury, Rochdale & Oldham Steam Tramways Co. This latter company, however, with 30¼ route miles, 91 locomotives and 81 cars operated no mileage at all in Manchester itself, and in 1888 the city's name was dropped from the title.

Liverpool and Glasgow, among the larger cities of Great Britain, both had extensive horse tramways which began operations in 1869 and 1872 respectively, flourishing until 1901. England's second city, Birmingham, however pinned its faith to the steam tram, and apart from some 30 horse cars working on 15½ miles of track, had little to do with horse traction. Only a very small portion of this mileage was actually within the city boundaries.

From 1870 onwards, horse tramways began to be established in towns both large and small, all over the United Kingdom, mostly operated latterly by companies under lease from the local authorities, while two very short examples, one each in Scotland and Ulster, were owned and worked by railway companies. A third line came under railway ownership in 1895, when the South Eastern Railway, which in 1899 became part of the South Eastern & Chatham Railway (SE&CR) purchased the Folkestone, Sandgate & Hythe Tramway Co., which never actually reached Folkestone. This had been inaugurated as a private company in 1879, but did not open its route until 1891-92, and the SE&CR continued to work it until 1921, even building one or two cars for it in the railway workshops at Ashford. The Scottish line was the Inchture Tramway, in the County of Fife, it was built to connect the town with its railway station, which was some distance away, and was operated with a single double-deck car by the Caledonian Railway. The Fintona Tramway in Co. Tyrone, had been built as the first section of the Fintona-Omagh line by the Londonderry & Enniskillen Railway and opened to traffic in 1853. When the Londonderry & Enniskillen Railway opened its line north-eastwards from Dromore towards Omagh in 1854, it joined the existing line at a point that became known as Fintona Junction ¾ mile from Fintona terminus. The short branch to Fintona, which this created, became a horse-worked tramway from 1854 until 1957, latterly as part of the Great Northern Railway (Ireland).

Several horse tramways lasted well into the present century, but only one of the long lasting ones - that at Llanelly - was ever electrified, in 1911. One, Douglas Corporation (formerly the Isle of Man Tramways Co.) is still in use, and is now the sole surviving horse tramway in the British Isles. The other long-service tramways were mainly in England; the Morecambe Tramways Co. operated until 1908, when it was purchased by the Corporation, who replaced it with municipal motor buses in 1926. Coming to within 10 yards of the Morecambe line, though never being joined to it, was the system of the Lancaster & District Tramways Co. Ltd, which worked a line from the city of Lancaster to Morecambe until 1921. It was then replaced by motor buses of a predecessor of Ribble Motor Services, though Lancaster Corporation operated some local urban services with electric cars contemporaneously. The Brighton &

The real centre of the huge city of Liverpool, difficult really to define exactly, is perhaps what we see here. We are in Lime Street, looking north, in about 1890. The North-Western Hotel is on the right, with, behind it, the main Lime Street terminal station of the London & North Western Railway. On the extreme left is St George's Hall, also the Wellington Monument, whilst the bottom left corner leads to St John's Lane. We see a vast array of Liverpool United Tramways & Omnibus Co. Ltd horse trams, at least eight. By now they all have only six windows each side, whereas early trams from most manufacturers usually had seven or eight, although smaller. The tram in the foreground, which gives a good view of upper-deck knifeboard seating, is standing on the terminal siding, in The Quadrant, of the service to and from Bootle.

Photomatic

Lime Street again, but from a slightly different viewpoint. less of the North Western Hotel, more of St George's Hall, and only six Liverpool United Tramways & Omnibus Co. Ltd trams instead of eight; with the Free Library and Walker Art Gallery in the distance. The three trams in the foreground are all terminating on the Bootle service, and we can see their knifeboard seats on top. Close alongside are three horse-drawn cabs also waiting for passengers. The date is again somewhere about 1890.

Photomatic

This Liverpool United Tramways & Omnibus Co. Ltd car is bound, in 1886, for the Pier Head, the main terminus by the riverside with its cross-Mersey ferries, which in horse days had only one large turning circle but in later (electric) days became famous for having three. Trams worked inwards via Church Street and James Street, and outwards via Water Street and Dale Street. There was competition here, though we cannot see it, for the Mersey Railway, constructed in 1884-85, ran in tunnel underneath Church Street and James Street. *Photomatic*

A Liverpool United Tramways & Omnibus Co. Ltd two-horse open-topped car is at the entrance to the depot at West Derby terminus, on the west side of The Square, next to the Manor Court House. A ramp at the rear gave access to the stables on the first floor, and a hay loft was on the second floor. The car is of the patent Eades reversible type, and it has no staircase at the front. The Liverpool company built many of its tramcars in its own factory at Aigburth, and later at Lambeth Road, but there is no evidence that this particular one was so built.   *Photomatic*

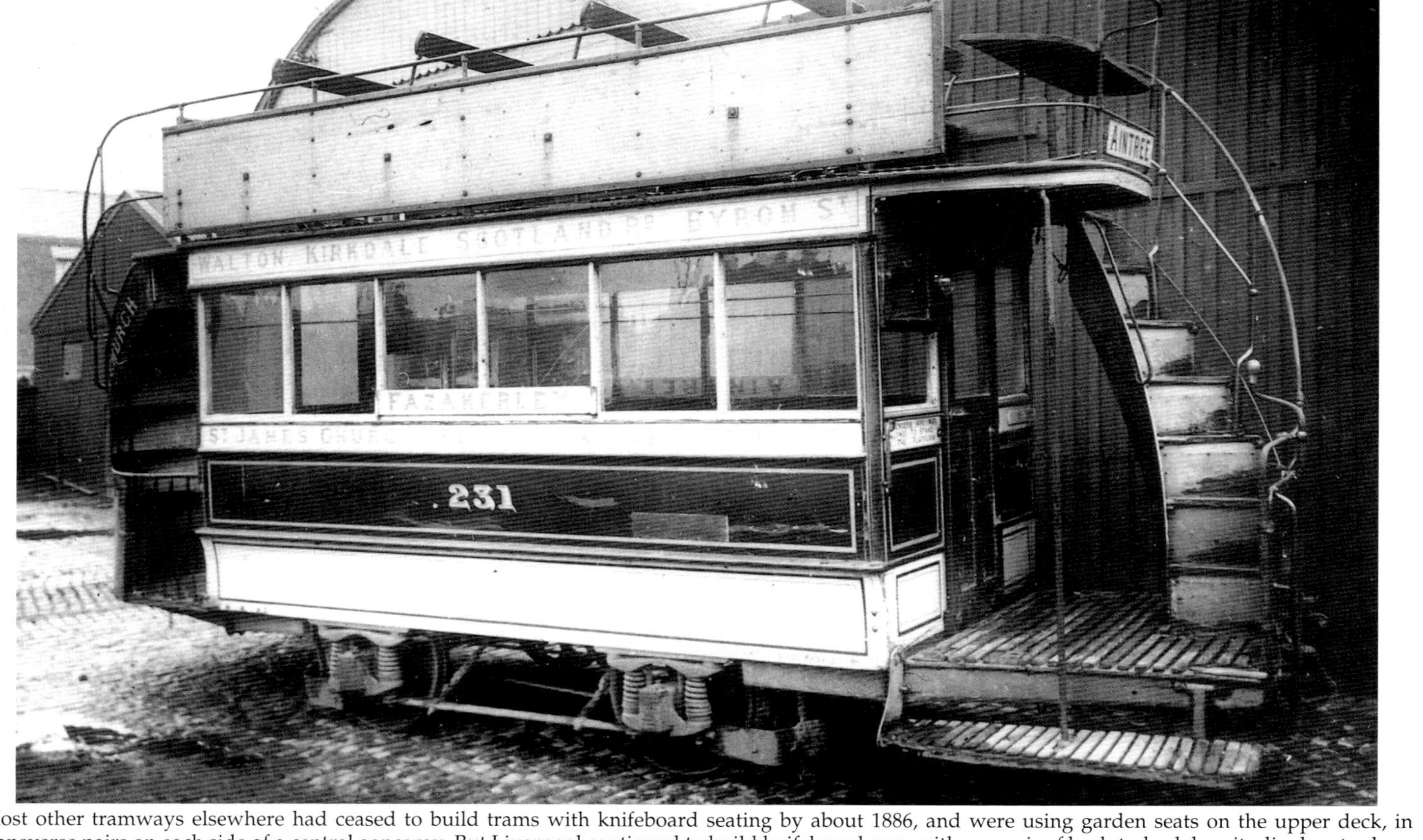

Most other tramways elsewhere had ceased to build trams with knifeboard seating by about 1886, and were using garden seats on the upper deck, in transverse pairs on each side of a central gangway. But Liverpool continued to build knifeboard cars, with one pair of back-to-back longitudinal seats along the full length of the centre of the top deck. Liverpool United Tramways did not have any garden-seat cars until 1892, and even then, only very few. Here we see car No. 231, one of the first few built in 1892, photographed in 1901 after being withdrawn from service for electrification, and meanwhile repainted in the livery of Liverpool Corporation which had acquired the company in 1897. The car displays route information for the Fazakerley to Lime Street service.

The Folkestone, Sandgate & Hythe Tramways Co., which did not actually serve Folkestone, despite intending to, owned a 3⅓ mile horse tramway from St Paul's Church, Sandgate, along the High Street, Esplanade, and Prince's Road, which was opened as far as the Seabrook Hotel on 18th May, 1891, and extended to the Red Lion at Hythe on 6th June, 1892. The hotel was owned by Sir Edward Watkin, Chairman of the South Eastern Railway, and by Act of 29th June, 1893 the South Eastern Railway purchased the tramway company. The depot was at the Hythe terminus, and there were two open toast rack cars, two closed toast racks, and one saloon car. Here in 1903 we see one of them in Sandgate High Street, well loaded, with two passengers on the outside footboard. The line survived until the autumn of 1921, one of the very few horse tramways to keep open as late as that. In the far distance we can see the top of the Sandgate Hill Cliff Lift, whose bottom was just opposite the tram terminus.

Photomatic

The Folkestone, Sandgate & Hythe Tramways Co., which never did reach its intended terminus, was one of the smallest. One of the company's open cars is shown here, on the Promenade near the Sandgate end of the line, close to the pavement. The entire route was single track, with only four passing loops, hence for much of the way eastbound trams were on the wrong side of the road for other traffic.

Pamlin Prints

The Folkestone, Sandgate & Hythe Tramways Co. had only one enclosed saloon car, and here it is. Four other cars were all of toast rack layout. We are here at the Hythe terminus at the Red Lion Hotel, and the tram depot is just off the picture to the right. The South Eastern Railway and the London, Chatham & Dover Railway amalgamated in 1899 to become the South Eastern & Chatham Railways. This photograph must have been taken after that date, because the car is lettered 'SE&CR' and not 'SER'.

Author's Collection

The Isle of Man Tramways Ltd horse tramway along the seafront at Douglas, was originally opened in two sections in 1876-77 by Thomas Lightfoot. He sold it in 1882 to a new Isle of Man Tramways Ltd, who in 1894 sold it to the Isle of Man Tramways & Electric Power Co. Ltd, and then in 1902 the line was purchased by Douglas Corporation, who still own and operate it more than a century later. Our photograph was probably taken immediately after the take-over by the Isle of Man Tramways in 1882, the words 'The Douglas Bay Tramways' can be seen on the lower panel of the car, behind the three standing people. This car is No. 4 built in 1882 by Starbuck, with 32 seats, and scrapped in 1949. With the absence of any panelling around the sides of the upper deck we can see more clearly what knifeboard seating looked like.

Author's Collection

Douglas Corporation Transport purchased in 1902 the horse tramway along the local Promenade which had been constructed in three sections 1876/77/89. At least 47 of the maximum fleet of 50 cars were built during 1876 to 1911 in about 16 batches or body styles from five different manufacturers, and about a half of them still survive today. Four cars are enclosed saloon single-deckers, and all the other single-deckers are, or were, various types of toast rack cars. No. 36, seen here, was built in 1894 by Milnes with eight five-seat benches.

Punch Bowl Press

The Brighton & Shoreham Tramway Co. Ltd did not actually serve Brighton. Its 4¼ mile route started in Hove at Westbourne Gardens, and ran along New Church Road through Aldrington, Portslade, Southwick, Kingston-by-Sea and Shoreham to the Burrell Hotel. A further ¼ mile beyond here to the Swiss Gardens was abandoned only a few months after opening. The full 4½ miles was opened on 3rd July, 1884, and all except Swiss Gardens survived until 23rd May, 1908. At first it was a steam tramway, worked with locomotives and eight-wheel double-deck cars, but these proved too heavy for the track and after some years they were abandoned and replaced by horses. By the end of 1889 there were five single-deck horse cars and two double-deckers, apparently all built by the Oldbury Railway Carriage & Wagon Co. Ltd. After closure the British Electric Traction Co. Ltd purchased the company, hoping to electrify it, and in order to keep the legal rights alive the tramway was re-opened on 10th June, 1910 with a skeleton service worked by one horse tram only, namely No. 10. The line finally closed on 6th June, 1913. Our photograph shows car No. 10 parked in the depot yard at Southwick the very next day, note the wreath hanging under the front canopy.

Author's Collection

The Morecambe Tramways Co. operated a 4 mile horse tramway from 3rd June, 1887 from Strawberry Gardens, Heysham, along the seafront to East View, Morecambe, later extended to Bare. On 20th July, 1909 about two-thirds of the route was purchased by Morecambe Corporation, but Heysham Urban District Council did not exercise their legal right to buy the remainder. Later the two municipalities were amalgamated with each other. The system was abandoned on 4th October, 1926. Until then these were the last horse tramways in passenger transport anywhere in England. There were two toast rack cars and 15 open-top double-deckers, all of which were built by the Lancaster Railway Carriage & Wagon Co. Ltd, whose factory was only four miles away. Our picture shows car No. 8 standing at the Bare terminus on the final abandonment day.

Alan Shackleton

A period picture postcard of a Llanelly Tramways Co. Ltd horse tram comically titled as 'Our Local Express, Llanelly'. The Llanelly system was built to a gauge of 4 ft 8½ in. and consisted of two routes, Llanelly station to Felinfoel, and Pwll to Bynea.

In 1911 Llanelly Tramways Co. Ltd was purchased by Llanelly Corporation. The Corporation electrified the system and it continued to operate as an electric tramway until 16th February, 1933. This photograph shows double-deck open-top non-vestibuled 4-wheel electric tramcar No. 1 in August 1931.

Shoreham Tramway Co. Ltd operated until 1913, though it never actually entered Brighton itself; the university cities of Oxford and Cambridge also had horse tramway services, which were abandoned in 1913 and 1914 respectively.

In Wales, the Pwllheli & Llanbedrog Tramway, on the edge of the Lleyn Peninsula, was still working in 1927, when it had to be closed down, as part of it was washed into the sea by a fierce storm. Pwllheli also had a Council-owned horse tramway from station to beach, as had Harlech further south. Further south still, the narrow gauge Fairbourne Tramway, a short line on the south side of the Mawddach Estuary, opposite Barmouth, worked until 1916, when it was converted into a miniature steam railway, and is still operating. Scotland's Inchture Tramway was closed in 1916 as a war economy measure, and never reopened, but 40 miles further south-west, the Stirling & Bridge of Allan Tramways Co. Ltd was still working until 1920; one of its cars was converted in 1913 to petrol propulsion, and it was intended to so convert most of the fleet, but this was never carried out, although the original conversion was quite successful.

Over in Ireland, five horse tramways survived into this period, the City of Derry Tramway Co. (1920), Galway & Salthill Tramway (1919), Warrenpoint & Rostrevor Tramway (1915), and the Glenanne & Loughgilly Tramway (1918). This last named, though 2½ miles in length, possessed only one car, and was built by the owner of a linen mill for the convenience of his employees, though it was also used to convey supplies to the mill. Finally, the Fintona Tramway of the Great Northern Railway was in use until 1957, and might still have been functioning had not the rationalisation of Irish railways taken place, which split the Great Northern between the Ulster Transport Authority and Coras Iompair Eireann, and resulted in the closure of a number of branch lines.

As later occurred with electric tramways, isolationism and petty jealousies between neighbouring local authorities hindered, and in some cases prevented, the construction of horse-operated lines. Local bodies could not make up their minds, vacillating from pro to con and back again, were often prodded in one way or the other by landowners and local gentry, who saw no reason why the common herd should have the amenity of cheap transport at their expense. Hence the obstruction tactics which favoured the private horse carriage against the public horse tram. Lack of capital support for such enterprises also militated against the tramway companies; local authorities were loth to spend the ratepayers' money - even though the ratepayers were in favour - and did their best to persuade the public against subscribing to the companies, a dog-in-the-manger attitude which was, unhappily, only too common. As a result, many opportunities were lost, and the tramway network with its ease of travel, might have been much greater had not niggling parochialism taken such a hand. One may quote as an example the Aldershot & Farnborough Tramways, which after 20-odd years of bickering, from 1871, with the local bigwigs, companies and councils, finally succeeded in constructing its authorised 2½ miles of track, but actually operated for only a few months - and that only sporadically - after which it lay derelict for years, and was finally dismantled. This was an extreme case, but there were many others which followed a similar pattern. It is perhaps significant that in the industrial areas, where the lower orders of society had a bigger say in local affairs, tramways of one kind or another flourished, as

The City of Oxford & District Tramways Co. Ltd operated horse tramways from 28th January, 1882 until 31st December, 1913 on the local routes. Two others followed later in 1882, all five radiating from The Carfax and totalling 6¼ route miles. For many years the total fleet was 12 single-deckers, but by about 1900 all had been replaced by double-deckers, of which by 1913 there were 19. Our photograph shows a double-deck car No. 11. A new company was formed in 1906 intending to electrify the tramways, but the powerful University Colleges objected to unsightly overhead wires, so the horse trams continued another eight years and were eventually replaced by motor buses of a rival organisation. The original horse tram colouring was a darkish red and white, but towards the end the white parts were changed to a medium green. Many of the local people objected to this new livery, but it was perpetuated on all the buses for many years.

Author's Collection

The Cambridge Street Tramways Co. had four short branches from the main crossroads in the city centre, totalling only 2¾ route miles, with six one-horse cars, which was opened on 28th October, 1880. There were at first two double-deck and four single-deck cars, but two of the four singles were later converted to double-deck, and two more double-deckers were purchased in 1894 and 1909. All eight were built by Starbuck. The tramway was abandoned on 18th February, 1914 and the company wound up, killed by the rival Ortona Bus Company, which now put on six extra buses to complete its victory. Our picture shows car No. 5 in 1914, probably taken on the last day, with the driver and conductor and four others posing.

Author's Collection

The Pwllheli & Llanbedrog narrow gauge horse tramway in North Wales ran for almost four miles along the shore of Tremadoc Bay. It opened on 1st August, 1896, owned and operated by Solomon Andrews & Son Co. Ltd of Cardiff, trying to develop the area for holiday and residential purposes, but on 28th October, 1927 much of it was washed away by a fierce gale and high seas, and in early in 1928 it was decided not to repair it. There were about 10 small open toast racks and about six saloon cars, some of which we see here at the terminus at West End Hotel, Pwllheli, in about 1925. *David Brewster Collection*

The Fairbourne Tramway in North Wales ran for not quite two miles from a brickyard just north of the Cambrian Railways station, south, then west, then north along the edge of the sea to Penrhyn Point, connecting with a ferry across the estuary to Barmouth. It started life in 1890 as a mineral tramway conveying materials for building a village of holiday houses. and when this task was finished it started to carry passengers in two open toast rack cars. Some years later a roof was fitted to these cars, as seen in this picture, where we are looking north towards the town of Barmouth. As a horse tramway it ceased in 1916, for in that year the track gauge was narrowed and it was converted into a miniature railway with steam locomotives, and in this form it still runs today.

Author's Collection

The Stirling & Bridge of Allan Tramway Co. Ltd opened a 3½ mile horse tramway from the village of Bridge of Allan, southwards to Stirling town centre on 30th July, 1874, and extended it one more mile further south to St Ninians on 29th January, 1898. Both parts were abandoned on 20th May, 1920 and were never electrified. At various different periods there were at least 17, possibly more, trams of several different types both single and double-deck, from several different manufacturers, not all recorded in detail, and including some cars bought secondhand from both Glasgow and Edinburgh. Our picture shows car No. 22, purchased in 1900 from the Edinburgh Street Tramways Co. Ltd. This one car, only, was fitted with a petrol engine in 1913, and survived until the very end with just a skeleton service for the last 3½ months, but genuine horse tram operation ceased on 5th February, 1920. *North British Traction*

witness Lancashire, West Yorkshire, the Midlands and Tyneside. Even in these areas, parochial bigotry was rife, and prevented several chances of joint operation over adjoining authorities' systems.

By the late 1870s, the horse tram had come to stay, but it had barely come into its own when steam operation was available, and after a short period of experiment, became an established fact. Many areas indeed never had horse tramways, while others changed over to steam within a short time. While the period of the horse tram lasted (with a few exceptions, as we have seen) from the early 1870s to the late 1890s, the steam tram had a somewhat shorter life, until in turn ousted by electricity. However, a mere handful lingered on, and indeed the horse tramway is not yet dead. Cheap and easy to maintain, outclassing both steam and electricity in this respect, nevertheless its slow speed and inadaptibility to hilly districts was its undoing. It was also very restricted in capacity, for there is a strict limit to what can be accomplished by one (or even two) horse power. Douglas enjoys a great superiority in this respect, for its level seaside route and its leisurely pace admirably suits the tourist, who is out to enjoy the invigorating sea breezes for the expenditure of a minimum of effort, the maximum of time, and a reasonable charge. The undoubted tourist attraction of the Douglas line makes one wonder whether Morecambe, the last major horse tram stronghold on the mainland, might have been wiser to have retained its seafront system, with the same conditions as at Douglas, but with the benefit of a slightly longer route. When one takes into account that at Morecambe, and also at Blackpool, with its sophisticated electric tramway, horse-drawn landaus in private ownership ply for hire along the sea front, and enjoy considerable popularity, the case for retention of the horse tramway seems all the stronger. It should be mentioned that two long piers, at Southend and Ryde, had early established horse tramways, later converted to various mechanical powers.

G.F. Train's step-rails, which protruded above the road surface, were unfortunate, inasmuch as their use did a great deal to prejudice the higher orders against street tramways. Had Train delayed his efforts a mere two years until the grooved flush-fitting rail had become a practical proposition, the story of tramways might have been quite different. The grooved rail took several differing (and ingenious) forms in its infancy, but it did lie flush with, or slightly below, the road surface. Over the years it developed into the solid girder rail which was necessary for electric traction, and since horse tramways needed only a light type of rail, this was the reason for the wholesale relaying of trackwork on conversion to steam or electric working. Roads, as we have seen, in Victorian times were mainly water-bound macadam, which produced a sea of mud in winter, and a veritable dust-storm in dry weather, to which was added the droppings of countless numbers of animals. The alternative at this period, found mainly in the industrial areas of the North, was the use of granite or sandstone blocks, known in the North as 'setts', and in the South as 'cobbles'. These were equally obnoxious, for though they did not produce mud and dust, and were much harder wearing, the steel tyres of vehicles produced a terrible din, and in wet or frosty weather they could be a slippery death trap. The addition of a pair of steel rails projecting above these mediocre road surfaces, as introduced by Train, was the last straw.

Ryde Pier Co. horse tramway was opened along the main pier at Ryde, Isle of Wight, on 28th August, 1864, and extended along the Esplanade on 1st August, 1871. The car seen here was built at Ryde in 1871 using parts supplied by Starbuck. The tramway extension was converted into a full-size railway and reopened on 5th April, 1880, and a separate new pier, solely for the tramway, was opened on 12th July, 1880, parallel to and alongside the main pier. The fares charged for the ½ mile pier ride were 6d. first class and 5d. second, incredibly high by the standard of those days. Horse traction was replaced by steam locomotives early in 1881, but returned to horses at the end of 1884, then electrified and re-opened in March 1886 with two electric motor cars, for which the Grapes car and one other former horse tram were converted and used as trailers. The pier and its tramway were purchased by the Southern Railway, who in 1927 de-electrified it and substituted two new petrol-driven railcars with two trailers. This car remained at Ryde until its purchase by H.C. Winstone, eventually being presented to Hull Transport Museum.

Pamlin Prints

Chapter Two

General Construction

As has been stated earlier, the first horse trams were built in America by John Stephenson. They were exclusively of the single-deck pattern (*Fig. 1*). Along with the J.G. Brill Company, of Philadelphia, these two concerns dominated the tramcar market for many years, until gradually a number of other builders came into prominence in the USA. Their designs were the dominating influence of all subsequent cars, and even when British manufacturers started business more than 30 years later, the influence of Brill and Stephenson was apparent. Train imported some half-dozen cars designed by Andrew Pallas of Philadelphia into this country in 1860/61, and though British builders altered details in the design, these cars set the general pattern, and over the next 30 to 40 years the design of horse trams both single- and double-deck changed very little in essentials.

No British builder, however, copied the enormous elaborate corner posts of Brill's cars, nor the very shallow and sharply curved rocker panels (*Fig. 2*). The monitor roof was universal; this was a means of ventilating the interior, by which air was drawn into the car through external slots in the side of the car above the windows. As a rule, a steeply curved internal roof was employed, with in the case of double-deckers, the seating placed on top of it. In the earliest designs, upper-deck seating was longitudinal, with or without a backrest, and placed back to back along the top of the monitor - the so-called 'knifeboard' seating - with a gangway down each side formed by the lower part of the monitor. This arrangement can be seen in several of the drawings. Only a few of the most recent (1895 onwards) had plain arc roofs. Knifeboard seating was abolished, or at least, much less used, from the middle 1880s, in favour of the reversible 'garden seat' transverse pattern, and to accommodate this, the more or less flat false roof was designed, to fit over the monitor. One minor disadvantage of this arrangement was that it increased the overall height by some 18 inches, though this was, in most cases, no great detriment. By the use of transverse seating, a slight increase in capacity was obtained. Rarely, if ever, was transverse seating used in the lower saloon, since the longitudinal seating down each side gave more room for standing passengers, and made the conductor's movements much easier.

Upper decks were almost invariably open; few cars had roofs over them, mainly in order to keep the unladen weight as low as possible. Lower-deck saloons had usually 5, 6, 7 or 8 windows (some Brill cars had 10). However, the number of windows had very little bearing on the length of the body, which was rarely over 14 feet over corner posts, and some single-deckers were as short as 11 ft 4 in. Two four-window double-deck cars built by Brown, Marshalls & Co. in 1895 for Perth, seated only 12 in the lower saloon, and therefore must have been little more than nine feet over posts. The general average length was about 13 feet. This meant that lower deck seating varied only between eight and 11 each side in general, and upper deck knifeboards usually duplicated the

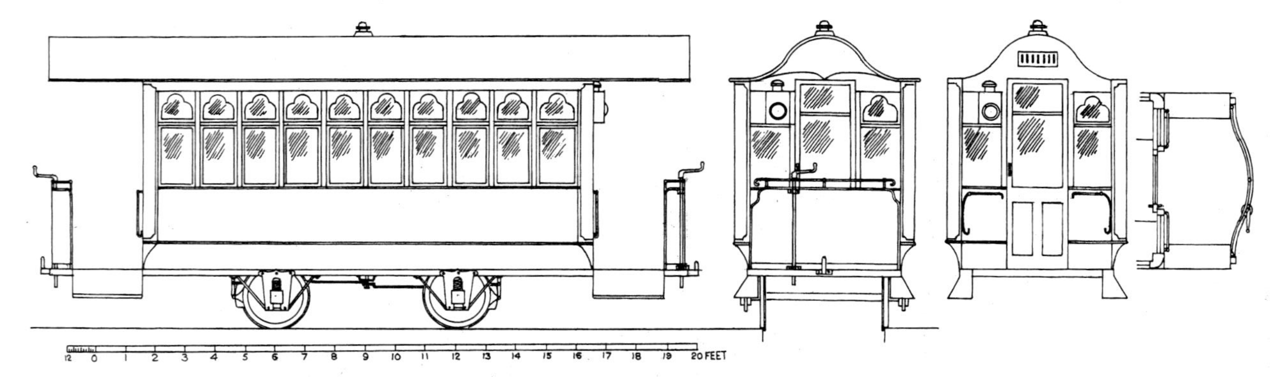

Figure 1: G.F. Train, 1860.

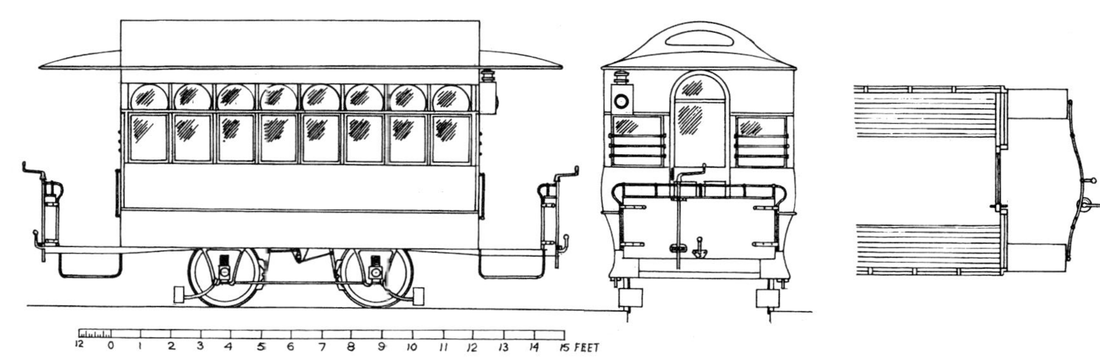

Figure 2: Jackson & Sharpe, 1864.

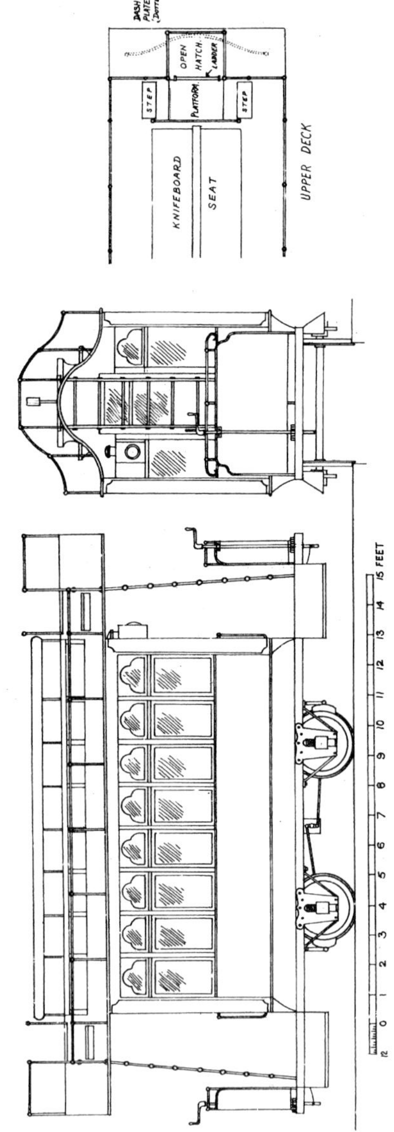

Figure 3: G.F. Train, 1860.

lower deck capacity. With transverse seating upstairs, space could be found for between 20 and 30 passengers, according to whether the seats were arranged 2+1, or 2+2. Open cars were also used fairly widely, with cross benches each seating four or five, and accessible from either side, with either fixed or reversible backrests to the seats. Some also had light roofs. These cars were generally known as 'summer cars', or more commonly, 'toast racks'.

In the early days, entrance to the end platforms was from either side, but later these were arranged to be from the near side rear only, the other side being closed off either by an extension of the dashplate or a separate iron grille. Some early cars had the entrance across the rear corner of the platform, but this type of access was more common with steam car trailers, though it was used on some early electric cars also, notably by Milnes.

Stairways on double-deck cars were, in the 1860s and 1870s, of a primitive character, either a straight iron ladder or a spiral arranged round a stout newel post which supported the canopy ends, the treads of these perilous contraptions being merely iron rods. A single handrail was usually fitted, though some cars did have the luxury of two. In the late 1870s the closed-tread stairway came into use, and these had a turn of 90° only, sometimes less. The double-decker was never popular in America, the large-capacity single-decker, whether horse, electric, or diesel being much preferred, even to this day. One is tempted to think that this point of view may be the result of experiences with the rattling, swaying Wells Fargo stage coaches of the Middle West. However, about 1858 Brill designed a double-deck car which was surely the most perilous and terrifying contraption of its time. Brill, for many years, stuck rigidly to his full-length monitor roof, unlike Stephenson, who made his monitors only the length of the saloon, covering the platforms with separate low-arc extensions. Brill's problem was how to get upper-deck passengers over the monitor, and he did this, not by copying Stephenson's low canopy ends, but by cutting a square hole in the high monitor ends and fitting an almost vertical iron ladder. Having got on top of the roof, the passenger had to make his way down the curved part of the monitor, with only a single handrail to help him, in order to reach the knifeboard seat. Later, to aid the descent of this slippery slope, a step was fitted half way down.

Safely (?) ensconced on his seat, the passenger sat in lofty discomfort, with only a 15 inch-high rail at the edge of the roof to prevent him falling off the swaying vehicle. This type of car was virtually a standard single-decker with a seat stuck on top. The upper deck was never used by the female sex, and it took the most hardy and adventurous male all his courage and determination to ascend to this precarious perch. At least two of these monstrosities were foisted on the unsuspecting British public by G.F. Train (*Fig. 3*). Starbuck modified the design by substituting a spiral iron stairway for the ladder, but soon cut away the monitor ends and put a low-arc canopy in their place, like Stephenson, which made the fitting of a proper stairway much easier. Another feature of Brill cars copied by Starbuck for a time was the top lights over the windows, which had club-shaped glasses. These he later modified to the much less complicated three-quarter circle which Stephenson favoured.

In passing, it may be noted that some years ago the author was shown a photograph of an early American electric double-deck car, in which the upper

Perhaps the most important street in Manchester was Piccadilly, and here we are, looking to the east, where the Manchester Carriage & Tramways Co. had a three-track section to provide terminal reversing facilities. The city's first horse tramway opened on 17th May, 1877, later than most other major cities, and Piccadilly followed on 7th May, 1880. By 1882 most of the system of about 87 miles was complete, but much of this was into other adjacent towns which were later purchased by other municipal authorities, leaving Manchester itself with only about a half. The city's last horse trams ran on 31st March, 1903. The four trams in this picture are all of the Eade's patent reversible type, as were most other Manchester trams, designed, and most of them made, by the company's Manager of its Pendleton workshops. On reaching each terminus the body could be rotated through 180º to face the other way, leaving the truck still on the same piece of track, hence there was only one staircase and one driving position, the same as an omnibus, instead of two of each, one at each end.

Photomatic

deck was reached by an iron spiral ladder fixed *outside* the body, in the centre – surely one of the most eccentric and dangerous aberrations to be encountered in that land of unusual things.

No horse cars had trucks, as generally known in electric practice. The axles were supported in brackets (or trunnions) bolted to the solebars outside the wheels. These trunnions were of various patterns, some with direct spiral springs immediately above the axleboxes, others with a spring on either side of the box, to which they were attached by lugs at the bottom, and these springs could be either inside or outside the trunnions. A few cars had a design similar to railway wagon 'W' Irons, with a leaf spring above the axlebox. Tiebars usually joined the bottom edges of the trunnions on each side, though this was by no means universal. Altogether, springing of horse cars left much to be desired. Wheelbases varied from five to six feet, with the former more common, according to the length of the vehicle. Brakes were applied by a brass handle on top of a vertical rod, almost universally fitted outside the dashplate, to the right of the centre line. To the lower end of the rod was attached a chain or wire cable which when wound on or off the rod actuated the brake shoes. A ratchet wheel and pawl, worked by the driver's right foot, served to retain the brakes in any desired position - this system, of course, carried right on through the years to the electric tram. The driver stood behind the dashplate, more or less in the centre, holding the reins of the horse, though in a few cases, notably the Eades patent reversible cars, he was provided with a seat. On lines which had to negotiate a hill, an additional horse could be coupled to the car by means of a hook fixed either in the centre of the side, or at the nearside front corner of the solebar, to give extra power. This 'trace horse', as it was termed, was held in readiness in charge of an extra man or boy, at the foot of the hill, and on reaching the summit, was unhitched and returned to the foot 'light engine' so to speak, to await the next car. The regular horse, or two horses for double-deck cars, had their harness attached by chains to a transverse wooden pole which had a socket in the centre to fit over a hemi-spherical steel pin on the front of the car, rather like the modern motor car attachment for towing a caravan. Occasionally the pole parted company with the pin, with chaotic results.

Wheels were generally made of chilled cast iron, with the flanges cast integrally, and could be solid, spoked, or with holes cut in to reduce weight. Axles were of wrought iron, turned to run true in the axleboxes, lubrication being by grease, in a somewhat hit and miss fashion.

In general, cars were of the lightest possible construction compatible with rigidity, since there was a limit to what could be moved by one or two horse power, and in consequence no bogie horse cars were ever constructed; bogie cars of large capacity only came in with steam traction. Oak or ash framing was employed, with corner posts the stoutest section, other posts and stringers being of the smallest possible section, ¼ in. or ⅜ in. hardwood panelling (usually teak or mahogany) was fixed to the framing. Sills (or solebars) were invariably oak. Generally a large colza oil lamp was fixed to the upper right-hand corner of the end bulkheads to give the driver a meagre amount of light in the dark hours, and these lamps usually had a clear glass at the back through which a pitiful amount of light penetrated the interior of the car. How the conductor

The Chesterfield & District Tramways Co. Ltd, in Derbyshire, owned Britain's smallest urban, as distinct from rural, horse tramway. There was just the one route from the town centre (Market Hall) to Brampton (Watton Lane) in the west, only 1¼ miles, worked with five (later eight) cars. This was opened in November 1882, municipalised in 1897, and closed on 20th December, 1904. We are fortunate, however, in that the only known photograph anywhere of an Eades patent reversible car actually being reversed is the one reproduced here. The many hundreds of Eades cars in Manchester, and many dozens elsewhere, all seem to have escaped the camera. Here Chesterfield Ashbury car No. 2 is being turned at the Low Pavement (Market Place) terminus, showing how all the bodywork, complete with the horse, rotates through 180° while the truck stay still. The horses had to do a lot of side-stepping to achieve this.

Author's Collection

managed to see to issue his tickets and make up his way-bills is a point not to be dwelt upon.

Reversing of cars at termini was a time-consuming business, since it involved unhitching the horses, walking them round the car, and coupling them up again. To obviate this, John Eades, of the Manchester Carriage Company, patented a design in 1877 which employed a separate frame for the wheels, with a circular ring plate attached to it, and having a pivot bolt in the centre. By this means, the whole body could be reversed on its undercarriage by simply walking the horses round in a circle. Thus, in double-deck cars, one set of stairs could be done away with, and the driver sat on a very short forward platform. A heavy iron draw-bolt was fitted, either at opposite corners of the body, or centrally on the driver's platform, by which the car body could be locked in place once it had been turned. A disadvantage of the system, was that the overall length of the car had to be carefully calculated, otherwise it might have overturned while being reversed at the point where the body was at right angles to the wheelbase. Both single- and double-deck cars were built on Eades' principle, and naturally his own company had a great proportion of them in its large fleet. Eades cars were also built by the Ashbury Railway, Carriage & Iron Co. Ltd, of Manchester, under licence. The Bradford Tramways and Omnibus Co. had at least four Eades cars in which the front portion of the upper deck had a roof and side and front windows, while the rear part remained open. Knifeboard seating was employed in these cars, which incidentally were intended for both horse and steam haulage.

In many cases, numbers carried by horse cars bore no relation to the size of the fleet. In some, the numbers were those of the licences issued by the local authorities to hackney carriages - for example the Stirling & Bridge of Allan Tramways had cars numbered 49 and 50, though the total stock was only fifteen. Unfilled blanks often occurred when cars were scrapped or sold, and conversely, if second-hand cars were bought, these often retained their original numbers, unless there was duplication.

In the earliest days, no lifeguards of any description were fitted in front of the wheels. It was not until the 1890s that any sort of protection was provided to prevent accidents to people or objects getting on the track. Even so, nothing like the Tidswell or Hudson-Bowring gate and tray pattern of lifeguards, as on electric cars, was used except on a very few cars which survived into the first 20 years of the 20th century. Even today, the Douglas horse cars in general have nothing more than four or five wooden slats fitted across the car in front of the wheels, though a number have in addition side protection of wire mesh on a light frame.

The earliest forms of lifeguard were primitive, and took the shape of either a blunt-pointed wooden 'cow catcher' or metal plates set at an angle in front of each wheel, to push objects away from the lethal flanges. At the end of the 19th century the fixed cross-gate of three, four, or five wooden slats, was suspended rigidly from the car frames but these, though probably more efficient in preventing some person or small animal from being run over, only served to push the object forward until the car could be stopped, with rather detrimental results. One thing which could be said for the primitive cow-catcher or metal plates, they did push objects entirely clear of the track.

The Bradford Tramways & Omnibus Co. was almost the only undertaking ever to have a covered-top double-deck horse tram, in fact Bradford had four of them, Nos. 16 to 19, built in 1884-85. Our picture shows No. 18. It looks dangerously top-heavy, and on narrow 4 ft gauge track, but there is no record of any of them ever overturning. One must take pity on the horses, for the extra weight of the top deck thay had to pull. They were built by the Ashbury Railway Carriage & Iron Co. Ltd, of Openshaw, Manchester, but under licence from John Eades, incorporating his patent reversible design, whereby the whole of the bodywork could rotate through 180° on a built-in turntable at each terminus, leaving the truck unmoved, so that the horses did not have to be un-hitched, and they also walked round through 180° with the tram body instead of changing ends. The body had only one driving position, at one end, and only one staircase, at the other end. Also the end vestibuling of the upper deck visible in this photograph, was at the one end only. These cars seated only 34 passengers, 16 downstairs and 18 upstairs, and lasted only five years. In 1890 two pairs of bodies were spliced together and mounted onto bogies, this becoming two eight-wheel steam trams instead of four-wheel horse trams, and now vestibuled at both ends of the top deck and seating 67.

Author's Collection

It must be said, as a generalisation, the products of different builders in this country showed very little individuality; the designs varied only in minor details, and it was often difficult to distinguish the product of any particular maker without a very detailed examination. The only ones to show any marked features, and thus readily recognisable, were those of the Manchester Carriage Co., and the Falcon Car Works. Windows could be straight or curved topped, ventilation slots varied in size and number, and there were slight variations in the shape of corner posts, but even so, it was difficult to distinguish one make from any other, as the same builder would often turn out cars with non-standard features, from specifications provided by the purchaser.

The gauge of horse tramways track varied from 3 ft to standard, 3 ft 6 in. and 4 ft being popular. Train's step-rails have been mentioned, and in the drawing included on page 46, a diagrammatic representation of various rail sections in use from time to time on horse tramways are shown. Some of these were ingenious, others primitive, and one or two were even reversible, so that a new section could be turned into place when the original had become too badly worn for further use, but these were rare. One of these was the Spielmann (*E*) but this was more common on the Continent. Following on the step rail, the Crescent (*F*) was used for a short period; this took its name from the form of iron section which was roughly a flattened crescent shape. It was spiked directly into longitudinal wooden beams through the running surface of the rail itself, and thus, after some time in use, became rough riding. The groove was formed by the sloped-off side of the rail, and was not popular for long, since the wheel flanges wore away the road surface which formed the inner side of the groove, leading to even rougher riding, and damage to the flanges. The 'M' rail (*J*) was used quite often in the 1870s again named from its rough resemblance to the letter M; it could have the groove to one side (which was much more common) or in the centre. Centre-grooved rails were used on the Liverpool and Wrexham horse tramways only, and indeed were never common at all, being employed for electric tramways only at Hull and Doncaster. This type of rail had definite advantages, in that it had two bearing surfaces for the wheels - which had the flanges in the centre of the tyres – and running was much smoother, especially with the later refinement of diagonal joints. However, the centre-flanged wheel was more difficult and expensive to make, which militated against its wider use. The 'M' rails were relatively easy to make with the primitive rolling techniques of the period, and were not difficult to lay, being spiked through each side into longitudinal wooden beams, which in turn were laid on cross sleepers, but its lightness made it unsuitable for anything beyond horse cars.

Kincaid's system (*B*) was a variant of the 'M' rail which was widely used; it could carry heavier vehicles, since it was spiked through the sides into a wooden block which in turn was bolted into an inverted V-shaped cast-iron chair embedded at its foot in concrete. The Isle of Man Tramways Co. laid this pattern of rail, and it was also in extensive use in Manchester, as well as elsewhere. Other systems which were developed in later years were Vignoles' (*C*), which was rather complicated, since it required special chairs and specially formed fishplates at the joints, making it expensive to lay and maintain, so it was not very popular. However, with bolts passing through rail, chair, and fishplate, the joints were very solid. A similar idea, which had a slightly bulbous section at the bottom, and supported in a cast-iron or concrete chair of rather large dimensions, was Crouch's system, in which an oak key was employed to tighten the rail in the chair (*D*). This was one of the earliest keyed rails to be brought into use - a system allied to railway practice. Spielmann (*E*) rails were not used to any extent in this country. They were an ingenious, roughly X-shaped design, divided into two identical halves through the bottom of the groove, being held in position in a rectangular box-like concrete or iron chair by wood keys. When the surface of the rail became badly worn, it was only necessary to knock out the keys and turn the rail over. When this in turn had become worn, it could be replaced by a further half-section, and so on. Though a good design, its section made it difficult to roll, so it was probably the most expensive type of track to construct, though it was capable of carrying heavier cars.

In later days, when the technique of rolling steel rails had become more sophisticated, Schneider & Hannay, of the Barrow-in-Furness Steelworks, developed the girder rail, with a fairly narrow web and broad tapered foot, which could either be laid in concrete or spiked direct to transverse sleepers (*G*). Thousands of tons of Barrow rails were used in this country, and abroad, both for horse and steam tramways. From this developed the British Standard rail, with slightly heavier head and a tapered web, the first being the No. 2 rail (*H*) which weighed 65 lb. per yard. For electric tramways, heavier BSS rails were produced, and became universal in due course. Bull-head rails of standard railway pattern, carried in chairs, were also used in some locations; its use for horse tramways was rare, but it was used extensively on electric tramways, particularly on reserved tracks away from roads. After the Tramways Act of 1870, the owning authorities were saddled with the maintenance of the road surface between the rails and for 18 inches outside them, which imposition was to become a great burden on the steam and electric tramways, and increased their running costs to a considerable extent.

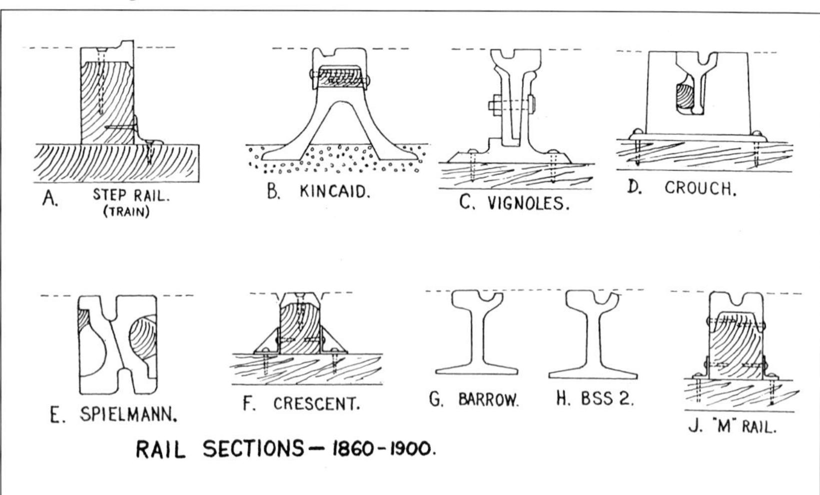

Chapter Three

Horse Car Builders

Vehicle builders in the horse car field were relatively few, at least, as far as the major firms were concerned. There were, however, a number of builders who constructed one or two cars only, mainly for operators in their own particular district, and received the orders mainly as a goodwill gesture for the benefit of local labour. Such individuals were numerous, but chiefly unknown outside their own circle; many of them were builders of coaches and other road vehicles. A few operators, the larger concerns, built cars in their own workshops, such as the Manchester Carriage Co., and the Liverpool, Glasgow and Edinburgh Companies. All these were in the end taken over by the local Corporations, who continued such building.

We have already seen that the first cars in the British Isles were inspired by John Stephenson. He also provided a number of cars from his New York workshops, including well over 300 for various London companies. Stephenson's designs were less flamboyant than Brill's, though they had points in common - both, for example, fitted dashplates which were shaped as reverse curves (*Fig. 1*) and waist panels considerably deeper than rocker panels. Brill fitted top lights over rather shallow windows, these top lights having peculiar club-shaped glasses, while Stephenson used a simpler design of either plain rectangular top lights, or a solid panel below the cant rails. He also favoured narrow corner posts, in sharp contrast to Brill's very broad, rounded pattern embellished with a wealth of scroll work. This, however, Brill abandoned within a few years. Both used monitor roofs almost exclusively, but while Stephenson's monitors were only the length of the saloon, platforms being covered by a shallow arc roof, Brill's monitors were the full length of the cars which posed some problems when double-deck vehicles were required. The result was probably the most horrible vehicle ever seen on rails. Though both companies built cars for this country, their influence on British construction was minimal. Another American company who built for English (and Scottish) lines was Jackson & Sharpe, of Wilmington, Delaware. At least two of their single deck cars operated on Train's Victoria tramway, and are illustrated by *Fig. 2*.

Starbuck Car & Wagon Co. Ltd, Birkenhead

When G.F. Train commenced his tramway in Birkenhead in 1860 one of his associates was another American, George Starbuck, who started building tramcars in 1862 at 227 Cleveland Street. On the formation of the limited company some 10 years later, in 1872, and the subsequent departure in 1863 of Train to his native land, Starbuck remained in Birkenhead as one of the Directors. In the 1873-74 he acquired additional warehouses in Cleveland Street, now occupying the whole of Nos. 227 to 241, which he proceeded to turn into workshops for the construction of horse cars and wagons of various kinds,

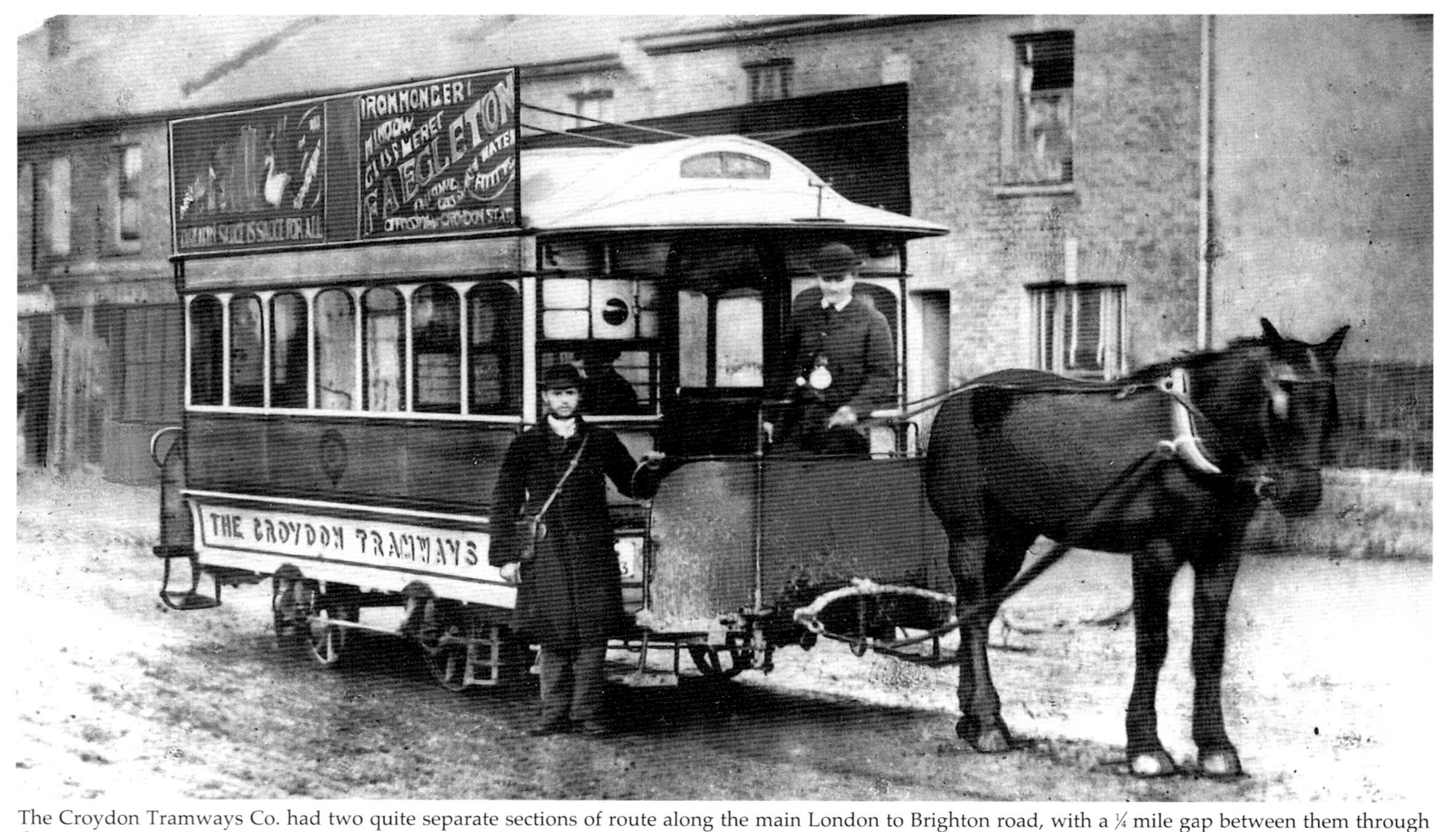

The Croydon Tramways Co. had two quite separate sections of route along the main London to Brighton road, with a ¼ mile gap between them through the town centre where the road was too narrow, and there were also three branches on the eastern side of the northern section, making a total of just five miles. The first section was opened on 9th October, 1879, and our picture shows one of the first four Starbuck cars of 1879 standing in 1883 at the Red Deer southern terminus of the route which was opened on 14th May, 1880. Routes to Norwood and Addiscombe were built by another company and later amalgamated. Croydon had 10 small single-deck cars, most or all by Starbuck, also some Starbuck double-deckers.

Topical Press

The Hoylake & Birkenhead Rail & Tramway Co. Ltd was one of three different companies all running horse tramways in Birkenhead in early days. It opened its one 2¼ mile route from Woodside Ferry (for Liverpool) straight along the main Cleveland Street westwards to the original Birkenhead Docks station (terminus of the Hoylake Railway) on what later became the Wirral Railway, on 6th September, 1873. Halfway along the route, at 227 Cleveland Street, it passed the tramcar-building factory of George Starbuck, which in November 1872 became the Starbuck Car & Wagon Co. Ltd. The Hoylake tramway was purchased in 1879 by the Birkenhead Tramways Co., and eventually electrified by Birkenhead Corporation in 1901. The Hoylake fleet was eight open-top knifeboard-seated eight-window Starbuck double-deckers, with a very flimsy open spiral iron ladder at each end for access to the top deck instead of a proper staircase. They were replaced in 1887 by eight slightly smaller Starbuck cars. Our photograph shows car No. 2 of the original 1873 fleet standing outside the Starbuck factory in Cleveland Street.

The Hull Street Tramways Co. Ltd which served most of the town although there was another company on the east side, opened its first route in July 1873, and by 1886 39 cars were working on almost nine miles of route. Here we see knifeboard car No. 15, possibly built by Starbuck in 1882, standing at probably the Beverley Road terminus to the north of the city. The company was forced into liquidation in 1887, but the liquidator maintained services until the Hull Corporation purchased the undertaking at the fairly early date (for tramway municipalisation) of 1st August, 1895. The Hull tramways were plagued by numerous railway level crossings which made timekeeping difficult, and also they used an unusual centre-groove rail instead of the normal type. The two most important routes, Anlaby Road and Hessle Road, were replaced by electric trams on 5th July, 1899, again earlier than most other municipal tramways.

Author's Collection

The Cork Tramways Co. Ltd, in Ireland, opened its first route on 12th September, 1872, connecting the separate termini of the four railway companies which served Cork with each other and with the city centre. There were six cars, all open-top knifeboard double-deckers. The survey which decided the route was made by George Francis Train, and the manager of the tramway company was James Clifton Robinson, both of whom appeared in the illustration on page 6, and the cars were built by Starbuck at Birkenhead. Here we see car No. 6 at the junction of Victoria Road and Victoria Quay in 1872, with the hills of Montenotte in the background.

The Cork Examiner

This is a view in Briggate, the main city centre hub of the Leeds Tramways Co. route network, looking north from the corner of Boar Lane in 1890. The tram on the right is probably one of the 32 to 51 series built in 1874-75 by Starbuck, based on the original Stephenson design, with 18 seats, at a price (for the first nine) of £167 each, and it is probably going to Reginald Terrace. The bus on the left with its rear door open, this being the terminus, is on the route to Burnmantofts, one of several small proprietors on this route, probably William Burnett. *Photomatic*

A rather jumbled state of affairs in Briggate, with several cabs and a barrel tank cart. The photograph was taken in 1892, and the Leeds Tramways open-top tramcar visible is one of the 21 to 31 series built by Starbuck in 1874 for £161.

The Aberdeen District Tramways Co. opened its first two routes, to Queens Cross and to Kittybrewster, on 31st August, 1874, but the Bloomfield route, on which the car in our picture is working, did not open until 1883. Eventually there were 10½ miles of horse tram route, worked by 39 open-top double-deck cars. These were mostly built by Starbuck of Birkenhead, but some were by a local Aberdeen coachbuilder by the name of Shinnie. Original Starbuck cars, with the then usual eight (or sometimes seven) narrow windows, instead of the later six or five wider windows, had only a crude iron ladder for access to the upper deck, which ladies never used, but the one in our picture has had a conventional quarter-turn staircase added at a later date at each end. The company was purchased on 27th August, 1898 by Aberdeen Corporation, who then built four open toast rack cars and purchased seven double-deckers second-hand from Liverpool. The first electric tram ran on 23rd December, 1899 and the last horse car on 2nd June, 1902.   *North British Traction*

having formed a separate company for the purpose on 12th September, 1871, which was reconstituted on 6th November, 1872 with additional capital and Directors. In due course, the Starbuck Car & Wagon Co. Ltd became the premier builders in the country. In 1886 Starbuck sold out to George F. Milnes, who had been the company's Secretary since 1882, and whose career will be followed next. Starbuck could be said to have been the father of the British horse car. His earliest designs were based on those of all three American companies mentioned above, but he never employed the ornate corner posts of Brill. For a time he copied the curious top lights of both Brill and Jackson & Sharpe, but soon dropped them in favour of deeper windows and a panel below the cant rail. His later designs set the pattern for other British makers, and apart from one or two who produced distinctive features, the products of most of them were only distinguishable from Starbuck by minor details.

In most of Starbuck's cars, though not all, the top rails of the windows were slightly arched, and the waist panels, mostly straight, were rather deeper than the rocker panels, which in turn were only slightly curved. His monitor roofs followed Stephenson's pattern. Early Starbuck double-deck cars were fitted with the open iron spiral stairs which Brill originated (*Fig. 4*), with a newel post placed almost centrally on the platform, but within three or four years these gave way to the slightly better open spiral placed on the offside (*Fig. 5*). A few cars supplied to the Hoylake Railway and one or two operators in Ireland had an unusual arrangement of curved window tops with very broad lintels, but this design was not perpetuated. It also incorporated a very low iron railing backrest to the upper-deck knifeboard seating, which looked (and probably was) very uncomfortable (*Fig. 5*).

Starbuck's later double-deckers after about 1875 were of lightweight construction rather than his previous heavy build, and had closed tread 90° stairs, some with reversible transverse seating on the upper deck. There was no great uniformity in his platform arrangements, some dashplates being flat and others curved, while the sliding door to the lower saloon was usually, but not always, placed off centre. These doors generally had semi-circular heads. Some open toast-rack cars were built, notably for the Isle of Man (*Fig. 6*) which had eight reversible-backed benches seating four each, and the front corner posts prolonged upwards to support an elliptical iron arch which carried the lamps. Two of these still survive on the Douglas tramway, No. 11 from Starbuck or Milnes in 1886 and No. 12 from the Milnes company in 1888. A peculiar aberration, seen only in two cars delivered to Wrexham, had the stairway at one end only, although the car was of the non-reversible type, and the stairway itself was encased on both sides with sheet iron, which must have made it very dark and awkward to negotiate.

From 1882 onwards, Starbuck began to supply bogie trailer cars for use on steam tramways, and was just getting well into this business when he sold out to Milnes.

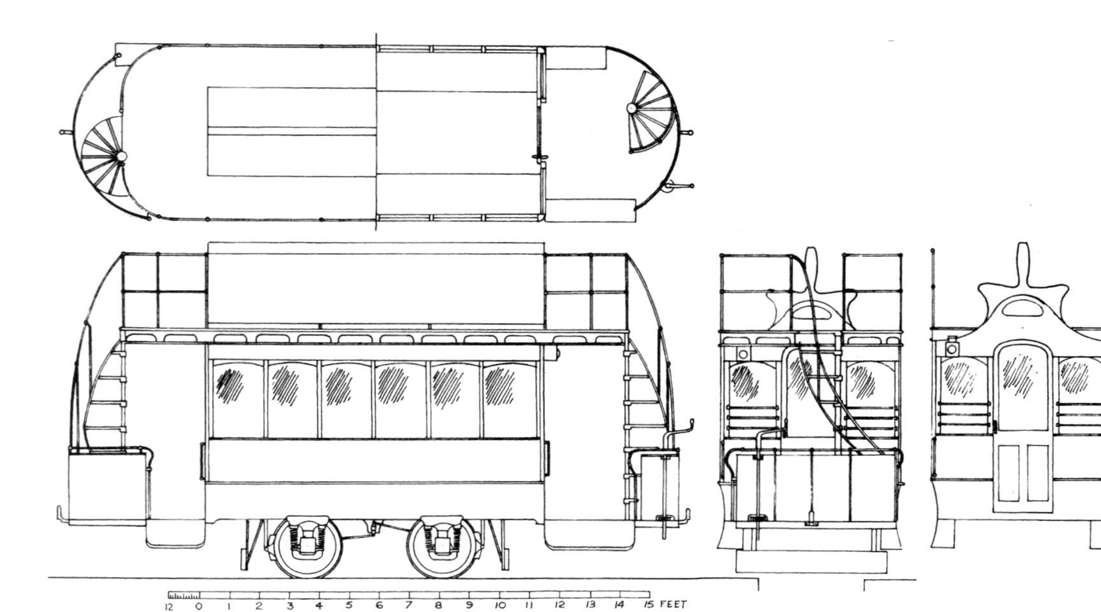

Figure 4: Starbuck, 1872.

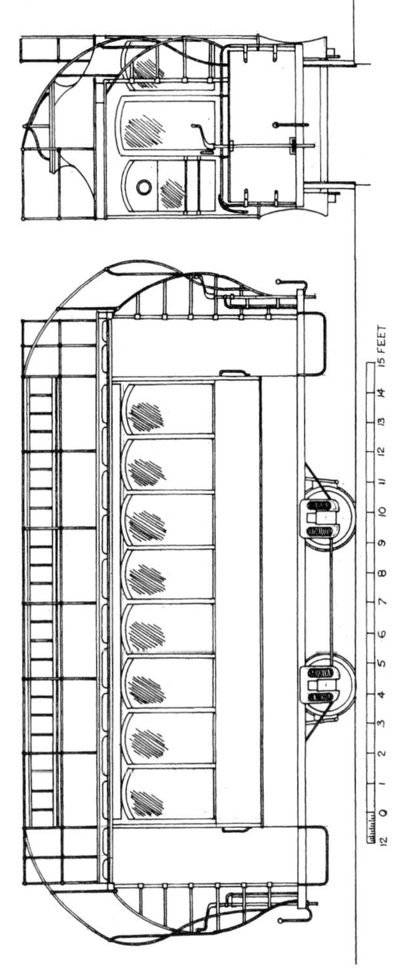

Figure 5: Starbuck, 1874.

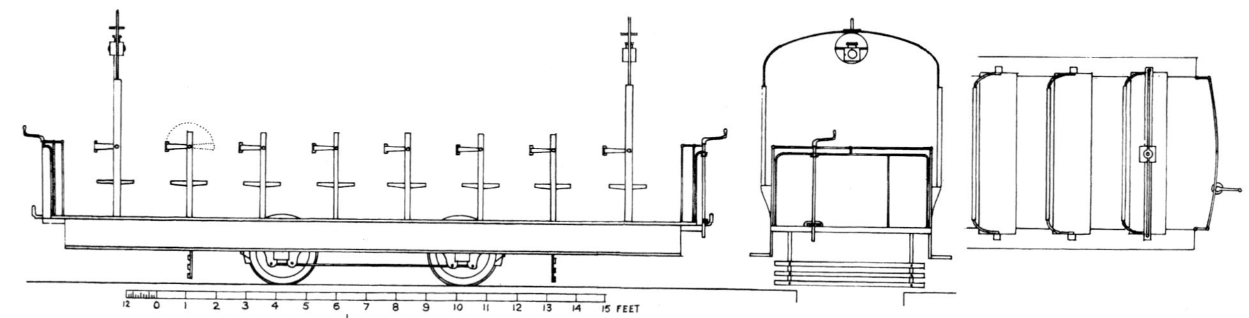

Figure 6: Starbuck, 1884.

George F. Milnes & Co., Birkenhead and (after 1899) Hadley, Shropshire

On taking over from Starbuck in 1886 Milnes traded as a simple partnership under the title of George F. Milnes & Co. It was 12 years before the formation, on 10th December, 1898, of the limited company, G.F. Milnes & Co. Ltd, when the word George was dropped. At first he continued basically the same knifeboard designs, varying but little from the originals, but very soon all his output was cars of the garden seat type. All other manufacturers soon followed, and after 1889 almost no more knifeboard cars were built anywhere. In the next decade, Milnes went into the steam car business in a big way, and finally in 1892 became one of the pioneers of electric tramcars. As business had expanded considerably, and being cramped for additional space in his Birkenhead workshops, Milnes decided, against the advice of his financial backers (one of whom was German-based) to erect a completely new works. He cast around for a suitable site, but nothing being available near at hand, he eventually acquired a plot at Hadley, Shropshire, where in 1899 he constructed his new works, which opened in June 1900. The move cost more than was estimated, and proved his undoing. His German associates were not pleased, and in addition, an engineers' strike in 1900 affected delivery of essential parts from sub-contractors, his position became precarious, and he was forced into bankruptcy in August 1903, in spite of having a full order book, and uncompleted vehicles in the works. The last trams were completed in August 1904. The assets, orders, and machinery were taken over by Dick, Kerr & Co. Ltd in May 1905, together with those of the British Electric Car Co. Ltd of Manchester (which was in a similar position) and together with its own Preston works, Dick, Kerr formed a new company, the United Electric Car Co. Ltd, on 8th June, 1905, and concentrated all the work at Preston where the few uncompleted orders of Milnes were finished off.

We have said that Milnes continued Starbuck's designs; minor variations there were, in that more of his horse cars had straight-topped windows, and he built only a very few cars with knifeboard seating. In some of his double-deckers, the side panels of the monitor were omitted, (*Fig. 7*) showing the double Y-shaped iron brackets which supported the upper false roof. He also introduced the 'Exhibition' stairway, which by steepening the angle, and only turning through about 75°, enabled a shorter platform to be used. This was a feature he employed on a large proportion of his electric cars, built between 1893 and 1904. Taking over in 1886, as he did, he was fully occupied with steam car stock, and built far fewer horse cars than did his predecessor, and indeed built hardly any after 1894. On double-deck cars the saloon doors were usually off centre, with semi-circular heads. Some single-deck cars built by him had monitor roofs with low arc canopies and five straight-topped windows (*Fig. 8*). These had elliptical-headed doors, placed centrally, and sharply-curved dashplates. Most of the cars produced at Birkenhead had waist and rocker panels of almost equal depth, but some special long single-deckers built in 1892 for Douglas (*Fig. 9*) had some unusual features. They had monitor roofs and eight arch-topped windows, with waist panels unusually deep. The platforms were longer than usual, having a sharply-curved dashplate, and a longitudinal seat for three on the offside of each platform. The monitor itself was unusual

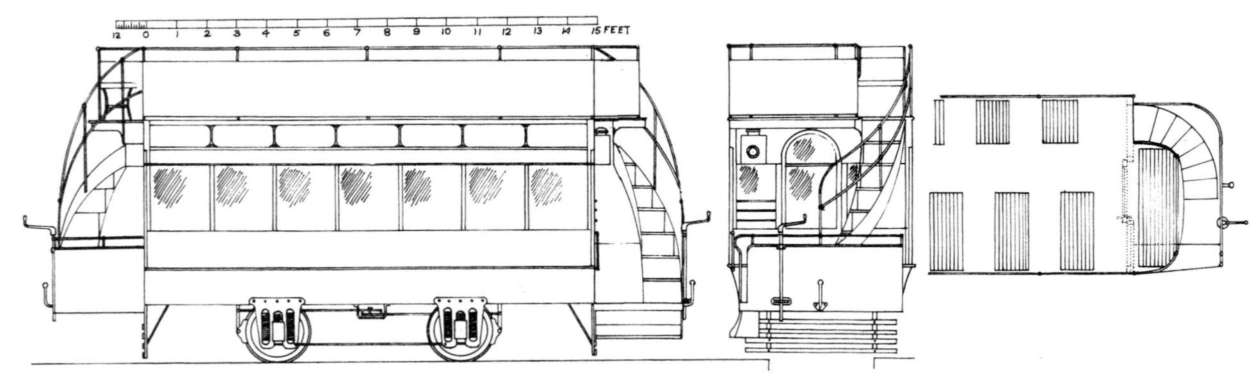

Figure 7: Milnes, 1894.

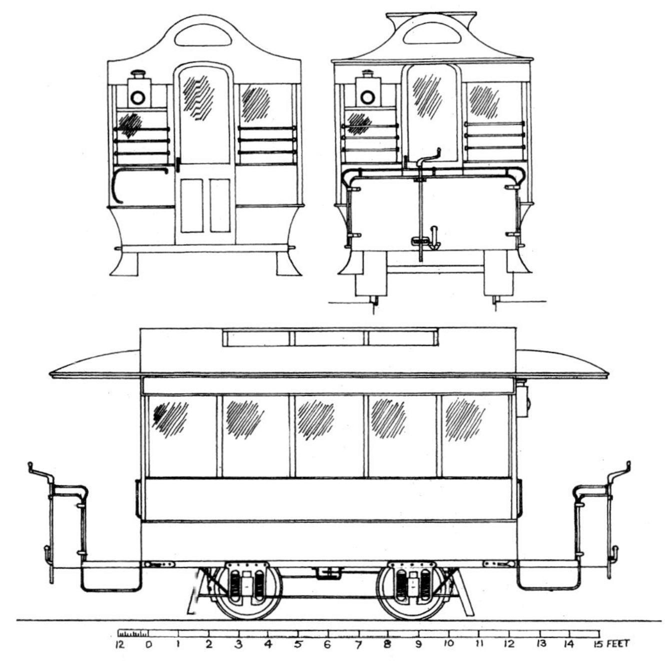

Figure 8: Milnes, 1888.

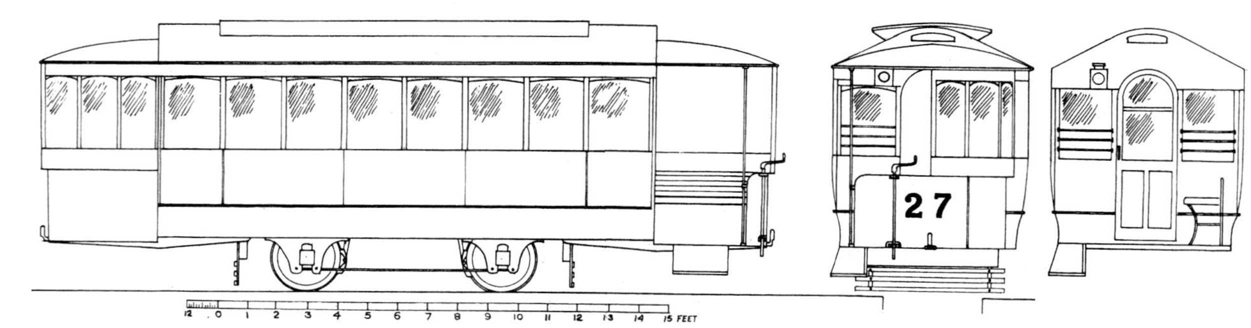

Figure 9: Milnes, 1892.

The Cardiff Tramways Co. Ltd was a member of the Provincial Tramways group which also owned the horse tramways at Plymouth, Portsmouth and Grimsby. It opened its first route on 12th July, 1872, and eventually had 6⅓ miles of route, mostly to the north of the town, with a maximum of 52 horse cars. one of which has been preserved in the National Museum of Wales. A separate company, which was owned by Solomon Andrews & Sons who also owned the Pwllheli tramway in North Wales, owned a 2½ mile east-to-west route which opened in 1881. The Provincial purchased the Andrews company (Cardiff & Penarth Harbour Tramway) in 1888, but their own tramways were compulsorily purchased by Cardiff Corporation on 1st January, 1902 and the Cardiff & Penarth Harbour Tramway followed in 1903. All were quickly electrified in 1902 and 1903 respectively. Our picture shows car No. 24 in the Provincial fleet, which, with many others, was built by G.F. Milnes & Co. Ltd in 1890, standing at the Roath Broadway terminus of the Newport Road route.

National Museum of Wales

The Belfast Street Tramways Co. started on 28th August, 1872 with six very short routes and small one-horse cars. This gradually grew into a dense network of 15¼ route miles and 61 cars by 1886, and 25¼ route miles with 144 cars, all double-deck, by 1900. Belfast Corporation did not purchase the company until 1st January, 1905, and the first electric tram was not until 29th November, 1905, with the last horse car 13 months later. Our picture shows two eight-window Milnes cars, and gives a good idea of the layout of garden seats, in transverse pairs with a centre gangway and reversible backs; the latter were tipped over at each terminus so that passengers could always face forwards.

also, in that instead of the common reverse-curve profile, it was curved only at the peak, the sides being straight. The doors had semi-circular heads, and were placed centrally. Later, Douglas Corporation added a half-vestibule to each platform to give protection to the seated passengers, as shown in the drawing, which depicts these cars in their final state. The driver stood to one side of the vestibule, which ended roughly on the centre line.

Most of Milnes' single deckers did not have ventilation slots in the panels above the windows; instead a narrow gap was left between the edge of the roof and the top of the cant rail, the window posts being slightly extended to support the roof. Built in different sizes, they usually had five or six windows. After the advent of the electric era, Milnes' production of horse cars fell rapidly, and the only ones built after the turn of the century were for Douglas. Probably Starbuck and Milnes collectively built more horse cars than the rest of the builders put together.

Lancaster Railway Carriage & Wagon Co. Ltd, Lancaster

This company was formed in December 1863 as the Lancaster Wagon Co. Ltd, changing its name as above in 1892. It was known more for railway work than tramcars, but nevertheless it did construct a number of vehicles of all three categories, horse, steam, and electric. Of the three, however, steam tramway trailers probably accounted for most of the output. The number of electric trams constructed was very small indeed, hardly exceeding 20 all told, over half of these being for Lancaster Corporation. Horse trams were built mainly for authorities in the immediate district - Liverpool, Preston, Lancaster and Morecambe in particular. Again the designs followed Starbuck's, and a typical double-deck car is shown in *Fig. 10*. This had seven straight-topped windows, with a low monitor roof and a long ventilation slot over each window. The seating on the upper deck was usually of the reversible transverse pattern, but a few cars were built with knifeboards. Waist panels were fairly deep, with consequently shallow rockers. Dashplates, though curved at the ends, were generally flat in the centre. Saloon doors had semi-circular heads, and were placed in the centre of the bulkheads, while stairs were of the 90° closed tread pattern.

Lancaster built very few single-deck cars, most of these being identical with the saloon portions of the double-deckers, but mention must be made of two unique open single-deckers built in 1890 for the opening of the Lancaster & District Tramways Co. These (*Fig. 11*) had side panels, and the floor was fixed at the top of these - producing what was termed a 'raised platform' car. The dashplates were slightly curved, and the seating, of the reversible type, was reached by a short 90° turn stairway of only four treads, on the offside of each platform. Raised iron railings were fitted for the protection of passengers. These peculiar vehicles may perhaps be described as squashed-down double-deckers. They were in service as summer cars almost to the end of the system in 1921.

Most of the company's output during the 1880s and 1890s consisted of steam tramway trailers, and, after 1902, the factory again concentrated on railway wagon work. The company became part of the Metropolitan combine in 1902 and was wound up, and the factory closed, in 1908.

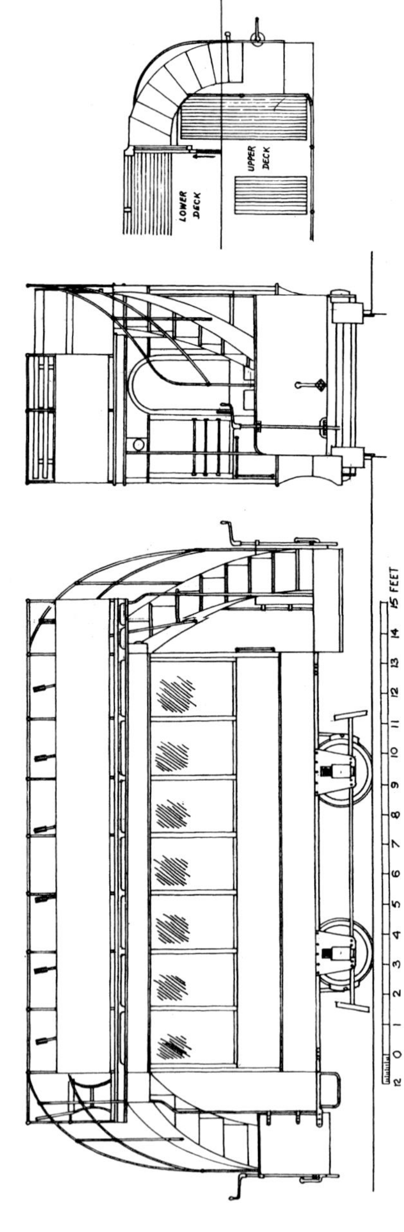

Figure 10: Lancaster, 1886.

The Preston Tramways Co. on 20th March, 1879 opened a 2½ mile horse tramway from the Town Hall to Fulwood via Garstang Road, with single-deck cars and 25 horses. On 14th April, 1882 an entirely separate system was opened by Preston Corporation, with three routes from the Town Hall to Fishergate Hill, Farringdon Park and Ashton-on-Ribble, totalling about 4½ miles, which were leased to W. Harding & Co. Ltd and worked with 25 double-deck cars and 92 horses. The earlier company sold out to the Corporation on 1st January, 1887, and thereafter the whole system was worked by Harding under lease. The lease expired on 31st December, 1903, on which date horse trams ceased to run, but electric cars did not start until 7th June, 1904, the gap being filled by Harding's buses. Our photograph shows a tram at the Fulwood Barracks terminus, probably built by the Lancaster Carriage & Wagon Co. in 1886.

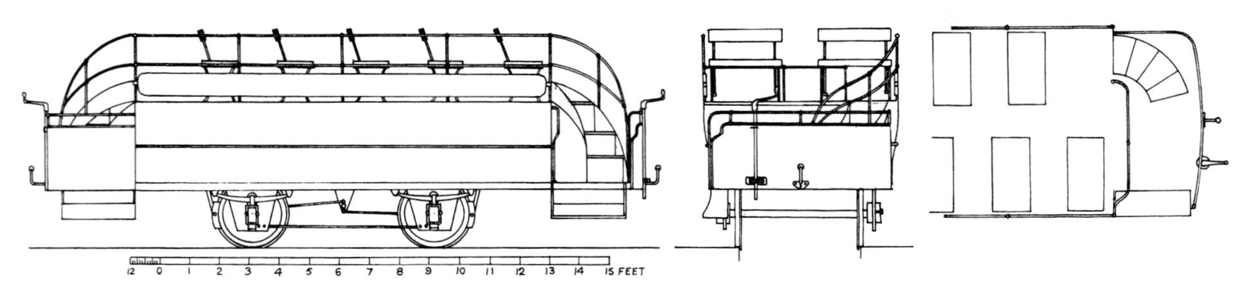

Figure 11: Lancaster, 1890.

The Lancaster & District Tramways Co. Ltd opened a 4⅓ mile horse tramway on 2nd August, 1890, from Stonewell, near the city centre, westwards to the separate town of Morecambe, where it terminated within a stone's throw of the local tramway system without joining it. It had 14 open-top double-deckers, built by Lancaster Railway Carriage & Wagon Co. Ltd, some of which were later converted to completely open single-deckers with an extremely high floor, as can be seen in this photograph. The line closed on 31st December, 1921 without being electrified, and was replaced by motor buses of a rival company.
Author's Collection

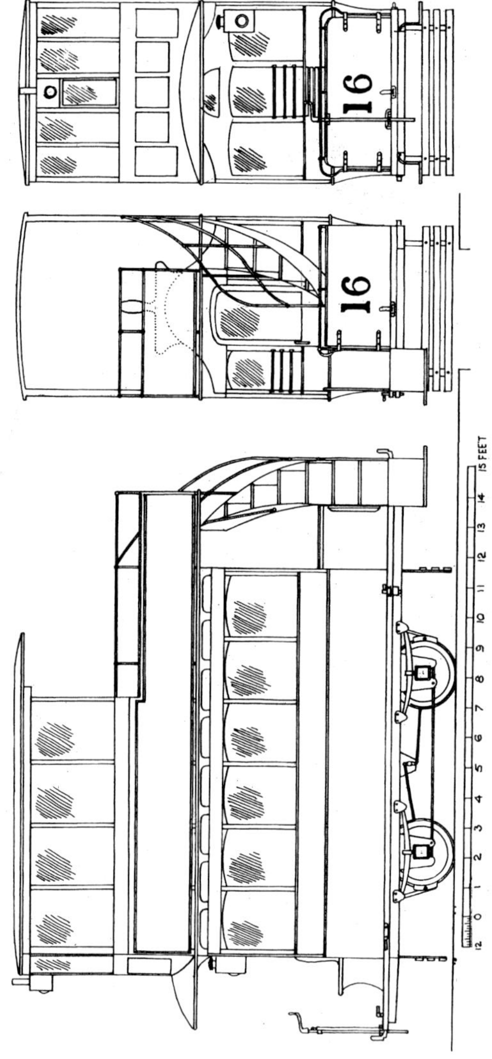

Figure 12: Ashbury, 1884-1885.

Ashbury Railway, Carriage & Iron Co. Ltd, Openshaw, Manchester

Another mainly railway equipment firm, which was also eventually swallowed up in 1902 by the Metropolitan company, they began their career at a very early stage in 1837 at Ardwick as the Ashbury Carriage Company, builders of railway carriages. In 1846 they moved to Openshaw, and the limited company - with title as above - was formed on 23rd September, 1862. The Manchester company dabbled in the horse car market, but like Lancaster, produced mostly steam tramway trailers. However, they did build a fair number of horse cars, mainly of the Eades type, under licence from the Manchester Carriage Co. (MCC), and their output was mainly double-deck. Four Eades cars were built for the Bradford Tramways & Omnibus Co. of a hybrid design intended for either horse or steam haulage (*Fig. 12*) which had the forward portion of the upper deck totally enclosed, while the rear part was open. Knifeboard seating was employed to reduce the overall height. As with most of the Eades type, they had the very narrow waist panels and deep rockers which characterised the design of the MCC. There were six windows with curved tops, and eight slots in the monitor roof. As the cars were reversible, only the rear platform had a 90° stairway, and the platform access was across the rear corner. The short front platform had a curved dashplate and a driver's seat against the forward bulkhead, which had three windows, with an additional ventilator over the centre one. A domed canopy was fitted over the front platform, and the upper deck had four windows each side, with five narrow windows in the front.

Although the usual bulkhead oil lamp was fitted on the lower deck, there was an additional lamp fixed outside above the middle upper deck window, which served to give a meagre amount of light to the top deck. The saloon door had a curved head, and was fitted off centre. Most of the company's other production was little different to Starbuck's design, varying only in the shape of canopy ends, arrangement of handrails, and other minor details. All had monitor roofs, and window tops were generally slightly arched, but some had straight tops. Few single-deck cars were built, and these were of the Eades pattern.

The company was taken over by Metropolitan in 1902 and wound up, but the factory remained open until 1928 making components for railway carriages assembled elsewhere.

Metropolitan Railway Carriage & Wagon Co. Ltd, Saltley, Birmingham

Beginning in very early railway days in the mid-1840s as Joseph Wright & Sons, this company became Metropolitan Railway Carriage & Wagon Co. Ltd on 5th March, 1862, and it was one of the principal suppliers of railway coaches to companies near and far. They did, from the late 1870s, onwards, produce a considerable number of horse trams for authorities all over the country, but perhaps more in the Midlands and South of England than the North. Both single- and double-deck cars were built, in various sizes, and with both knifeboard and transverse seating. Two of the smallest single-deck cars ever

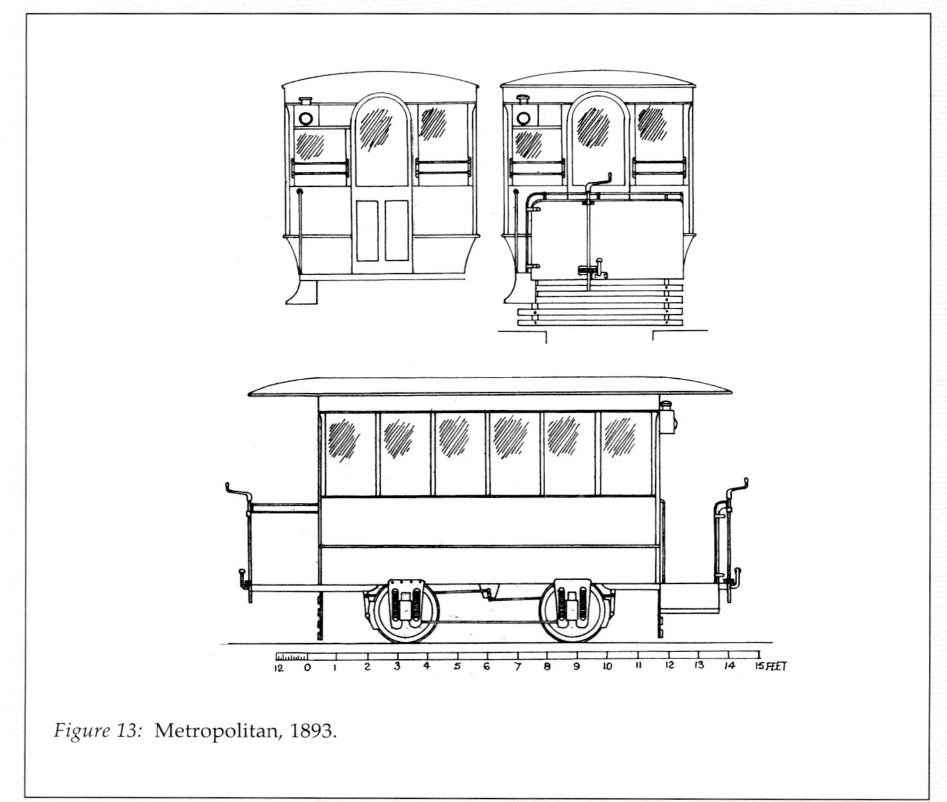

Figure 13: Metropolitan, 1893.

built, only 11 ft 4 in. over posts, and seating eight each side, were supplied in 1893 (*Fig. 13*) to the Birmingham & Midland Tramways Co. Ltd (B&M) for the Spon Lane shuttle service. This, and the Bromford Lane service, both in West Bromwich, were very short connecting lines between two main routes, and for many years were the only horse car services worked by the company. Though the B&M owned the cars, the working was contracted out to a Mr Crowther, who provided the horses and worked the lines. Both lines were electrified in 1901, and accounted for only 1½ miles between them, but were always worked as shuttle services. The two B&M cars had low domed roofs, without monitors, and six straight-topped windows, platforms open at both sides, and curved dashplates. The waist panels were fairly deep, and the centrally-placed saloon doors had semi-circular heads.

Double-deck cars were longer, the type shown in *Fig. 14* being a typical example, built in 1883. They had seven straight-topped windows, with curved upper corners, and had 13 ventilator slots of a rather ornate pattern. Platforms were open on both sides, with curved dashplates and 90° stairs. The elliptical-headed doors were placed off centre. Most double-deck cars produced were of similar pattern, with windows varying from six to eight, according to the length of the saloon. Single-deck cars were usually of monitor roof type, with similar bodies to the double-deck cars.

Along with Brown, Marshalls, the Lancaster, Ashbury, and Oldbury Carriage & Wagon Companies, the original Metropolitan formed a large combine on 18th April, 1902, with the somewhat cumbrous title of the Metropolitan Amalgamated Railway Carriage and Wagon Co. Ltd. In 1912 the name was changed to Metropolitan, Carriage, Wagon & Finance Co. Ltd, and again in January 1929. After amalgamating with the Midland Railway Carriage & Wagon Co. Ltd and Cammell Laird & Co. Ltd, it became Metropolitan-Cammell Carriage, Wagon, & Finance Co. Ltd.

Falcon Engine & Car Works Ltd, Loughborough

Although this company was, in 1889, taken over by Brush, which later became one of the 'Big Three' electric car builders of Great Britain, the Falcon contribution to the horse car market was comparatively small. It was founded in 1865, when Henry Hughes, an engineer and timber merchant at Loughborough, set up the Falcon Works alongside the Midland Railway to build railway and tramway rolling stock. In 1875 he built a steam tramway engine which was tried out on a horse tramway at West Bromwich, Staffordshire. This was the first steam tramway locomotive, as distinct from modified railway locomotives, on any British tramway. In 1877-80 he built 42 locomotives for eight different customers. Also in 1877 he formed a limited company, Hughes Locomotive & Tramway Engine Works Ltd, and he purchased a Stephenson horse tramcar second-hand from the North Metropolitan Tramways in London in order to study its design and construction. He then started to build similar cars at Loughborough, but this business did not prosper and in the winter of 1881-82 it went into liquidation.

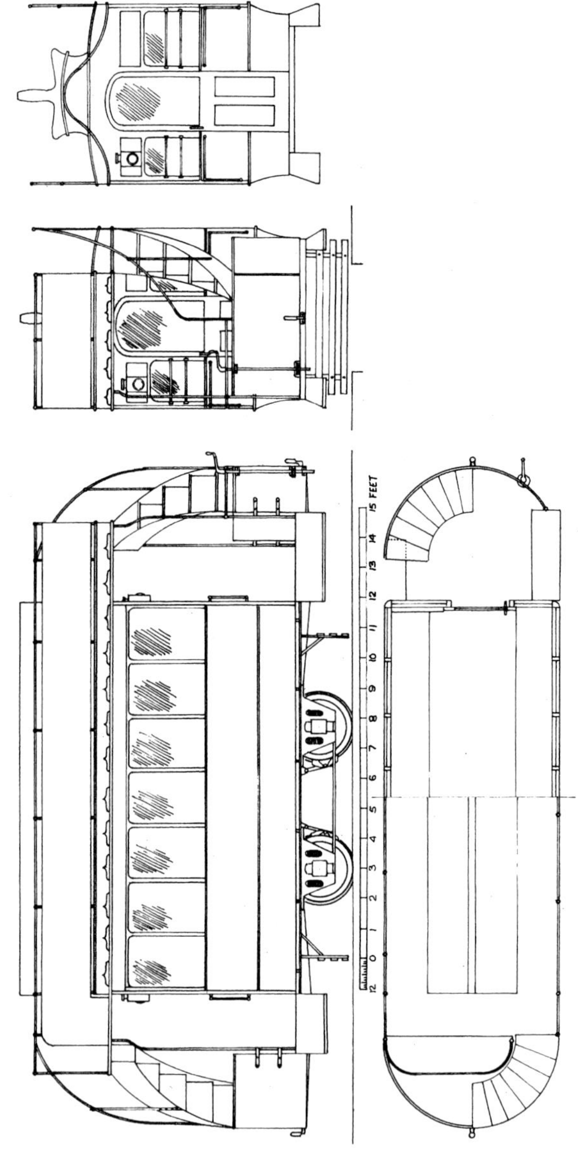

Figure 14: Metropolitan, 1883.

Hughes is thought to have emigrated to New Zealand, but the Falcon business was purchased by Norman Russell, who registered a new Falcon Engine & Car Works Ltd on 4th April, 1882. Russell designed an improved tramway locomotive in 1883 and built about 85 of them in 1883-97 for 14 customers, also about 80 railway locomotives in 1884-99. Until 1892 these were mostly on sub-contract from Kerr, Stuart & Co. of Glasgow.

Meanwhile Charles Francis Brush, of Cleveland, Ohio, USA, had invented electric lighting in 1875, and the first dynamo had been made by William Wallace in 1874. Wallace with others then registered in London on 8th January, 1879 a company called the Anglo-American Electric Light Co. Ltd, and in 1880 bought the world rights to the Brush system, and established a works in Vine Street, Lambeth. On 14th December, 1880 this company was reconstituted as the Anglo-American Brush Electric Light Corporation Ltd, with a capital of £800,000 (huge at that time) to take over the patents and inventions of Charles Brush. They moved into a larger factory in Belvedere Road, Lambeth, alongside the South Eastern Railway, and achieved great success in lighting public streets and buildings. Also in 1880 Brush invented the incandescent lamp, previous lamps having been of the carbon-arc type. Emile Garcke, probably the most famous name in the whole history of the British tramway industry, joined the company in 1883 as Secretary, in 1887 as Manager, and in 1891 as Managing Director. Progress was rapid, with the production of all types of electrical machinery, including alternators and transformers, and distribution of electrical energy over long distances. The Lambeth factory was obviously not nearly big enough, so Brush decided to find somewhere in the Midlands, and in 1889 they purchased the Falcon Works at Loughborough, with a very much larger factory and even larger grounds for expansion, a total of about 10 or 12 acres. On 10th August, 1889 the company was again reconstructed, now as Brush Electrical Engineering Co. Ltd.

At this time Brush was not primarily interested in tramways or railways, and was only concerned with electricity and its expansion, so they allowed the Falcon Works to carry on much the same as before, under the same management. Railway locomotives were still built but in decreasing quantities, until about 1910, although tramway locomotives ceased in about 1897 and horse tramcars in 1899. These products were stiill sold under the name of Falcon, not Brush, until 1899. Railway carriages still continued in larger quantities, and in later years Brush at Loughborough became one of Britain's biggest builders of bus and trolleybus bodywork. The factory buildings were greatly enlarged in 1898-1900, enabling large quantities of electrical tramcar bodywork and electrcial equipment to be made, with trucks as well following a little later. From 1877 until 1937 the Falcon Works built an estimated 1,800 horse, steam, cable, and battery tramcars, and an estimated 6,200 electric cars, giving a total of roughly 8,000; many of these were for export. Meanwhile on 7th November, 1895 Emile Garcke registered the British Electric Traction (Pioneer) Co. Ltd, to operate most of these trams, and this was re-formed on 26th October, 1896 as the British Electric Traction Co. Ltd (BET). From then until 1930 the Brush and BET companies were closely connected, and many of their Directors were the same people.

The Nottingham & District Tramways Co. Ltd opened its first two routes on 17th September, 1878, and others until 5th June, 1881, reaching a maximum of 10½ route miles. Eight types of car were bought from five different makers, until the last three, Nos. 36-38, came from a sixth firm, Brush, in 1895, of which we see No. 37 here on the Carrington route. The company was taken over on 16th October, 1897, by Nottingham Corporation, who electrified the routes in 1901-02.

Author's Collection

Thus it seems surprising that a firm so prominent in the electric tramway field should have built so few horse cars. Those which it did build were practically indistinguishable from Starbuck's designs, and were almost exclusively double-decked. Minor details, such as the fluting on the corner posts, and the arrangement of ventilator slots, were the only differing features from the well-tried earlier designs. However, in 1892 Falcon prepared a design which was submitted to the newly-formed Glasgow Corporation Tramways for approval, and one sample car was built to this design for that company. The Glasgow authorities adopted this design as standard and a considerable number of them were turned out. The Edinburgh Street Tramways Co. also adopted the same design, with the slight variation that in a number of batches they substituted wood slat ventilators alternately with the glass top lights.

Fig. 15 shows the design adopted by the Glasgow Corporation. These cars had six windows with rounded upper corners and a low arc roof, the monitor being discarded in favour of a low internal clerestory to give internal ventilation. Each window had a single fixed top light. Saloon doors had elliptical heads and a transom across the upper part, dividing the glass into two. Platforms were open at one side only, the other side, under the stairs, being closed off by an iron grille, though later cars built by the company had the dashplate continued to the corner post. 90° stairs were fitted and the upper-deck seating was of the reversible type. Variations on the design were the fitting of seven or eight windows, though for the bulk of the stock Glasgow favoured the original six, and Edinburgh seven. Building of these standard cars was continued by Glasgow Corporation, and a number of them were later fitted up for electric working, surviving for more than 20 years. One horse car, Glasgow 543, has been preserved in original condition. The Brush company is still flourishing today, at Loughborough, with a huge factory making many different electrical engineering products.

Brown, Marshalls & Co. Ltd, Adderley Park, Birmingham

This company started as a builder of stage coaches and later specialised in railway coaches, which were constructed from the very early 1840s. The limited company, Brown, Marshalls & Co. Ltd, was formed on 17th June, 1870 to take over the partnership of Broan & Marshall. In due course, they jumped on the bandwagon and tried their hand at horse cars, in the early 1880s, going on to steam trailers, and in 1892 to electric cars, though of the last-mentioned they built very few. The firm is perhaps best known for the large batch of 120 cable cars constructed around the turn of the century for Edinburgh. Most of these cable cars survived to be converted to electric propulsion in 1919-22. Along with their neighbours, the Oldbury Railway Carriage & Wagon Co. Ltd, they became part of the Metropolitan combine in 1902. The factory closed in 1908 and was sold in 1911 to the Wolseley Car Company.

Brown, Marshalls built all types of horse trams, single and double deck, also a small number of open toast racks. Their designs were characterised by a rather plain appearance, devoid of the wealth of mouldings and other embellishments

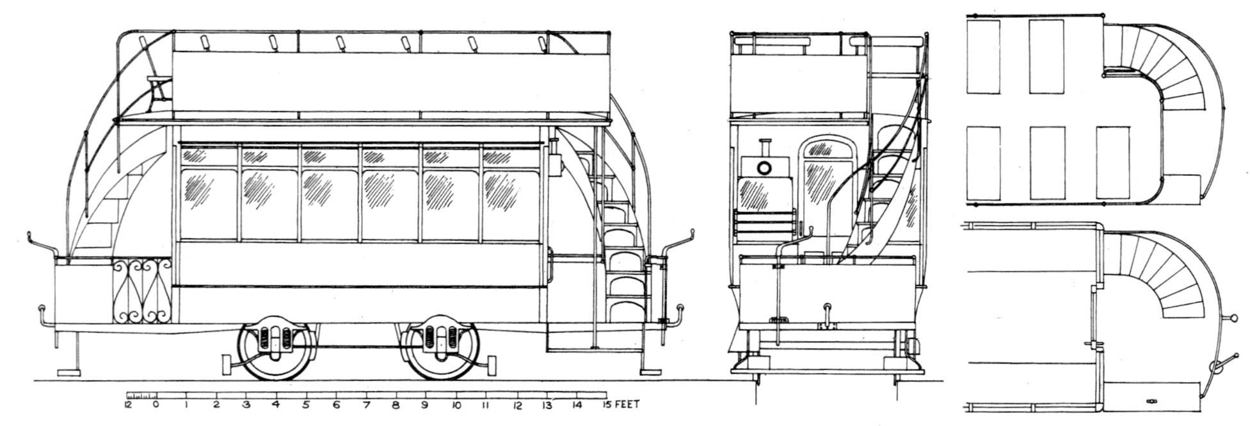

Figure 15: Falcon, 1893.

The Sunderland Tramways Co. opened its first route, in fact three of them, on 11th June, 1879. This photograph probably shows car No. 1, which was probably built by Brown, Marshalls & Co. Ltd of Birmingham. Upper-deck seating was of knifeboard pattern, with a medium-height iron rail as backrest, and a transverse seat for two on the end of each canopy.   *Pamlin Prints*

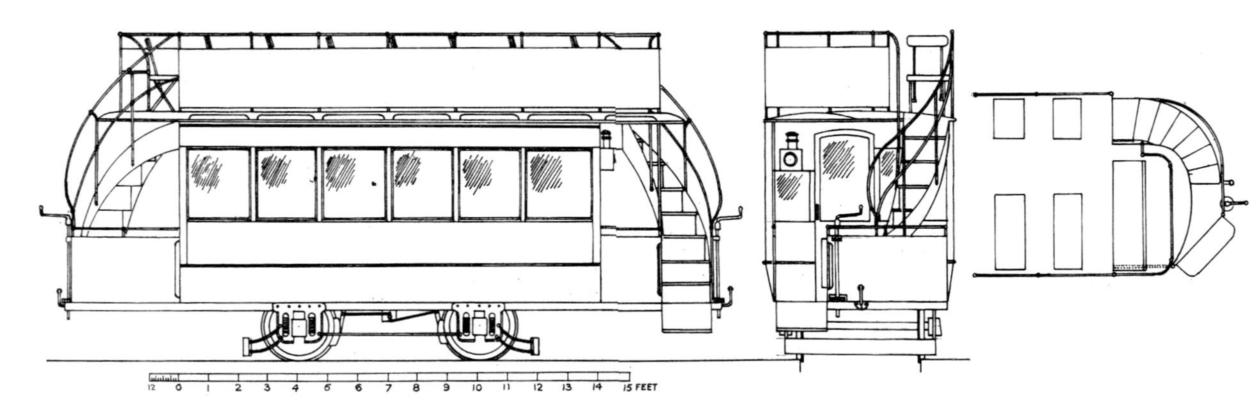

Figure 16: Brown, Marshall, 1890.

which other builders included. Coming into the field rather late, they built very few deep-monitor roofed cars, most of their output being arc-roofed double-deckers with a low internal clerestory. A typical car of 1890 is illustrated by *Fig. 16*, which shows six straight-topped windows and deep cant rail panels, in which were placed one long ventilator slot over each window. Reversible seating was fitted on the upper deck, and in a few cases in the saloon also. The platforms had corner access and flat dashplates which were sharply curved into the offside. The waist panels were usually straight, and slightly deeper than the rocker panels. Saloon doors were off centre, and had curved tops. *Fig. 17* shows a later car with similar features, but unusual in having only three windows, which had rounded top corners. There were nine ventilator slots, three over each window, and the doors with semi-circular heads were on the centre line. Waist and rocker panels were equal in depth. These cars were practically duplicates of the Edinburgh cable cars, except that the latter had longer platforms to accommodate the cable grip mechanism.

An unusual toast rack design was produced, of which only a very small number were built. One of these found its way eventually to the Stirling & Bridge of Allan Tramways, though its original owner is doubtful; it could have come from Edinburgh, as several of the Stirling fleet did. This car had eight fixed benches, back to back in pairs, the end panels being rather curiously shaped and with a large circular cutout in the centre, probably to reduce weight and having unusually high side rails shaped as reverse curves (*Fig.18*).

Midland Railway Carriage & Wagon Co. Ltd, Birmingham, and later Shrewsbury

Another railway construction company, which originated probably in 1844, becoming the Midland Waggon Co. Ltd in 1859, and the Midland Railway Carriage & Wagon Co. Ltd in September 1877. This eventually came into the Metropolitan fold, although not until 27th August, 1929, and then it was kept as a separate subsidiary company. Manufacturing ceased in 1929, but wagon hire continued until 1948, and the company was not fully absorbed into Metro-Cammell until 19th March, 1948. They did not do much in the horse tramway field, and still less with steam cars, but did produce a fair number of electric trams over a short period in the early 1900s. Their horse tram designs closely followed early Starbuck. The company was very partial to arch-topped windows, which characterised most of their electric cars, particularly for Blackpool and the Potteries. The horse car shown in *Fig. 19* was built about 1879, and showed several features of contemporary Starbuck, including the curved moulding at the ends of the waist panels, which Starbuck used occasionally. Apart from the closed tread stairs, this design shows a great affinity with Isle of Man Tramways No. 2, which Starbuck built in 1876. It had six arched-topped windows, platforms open on both sides, and curved dashplates. The upper deck decency boards were raised well above the floor. Later cars omitted the curved waist panel mouldings. Long before joining the other companies in the Metropolitan combine in 1929, tramway work was dropped entirely from 1923. The 1864 factory at Saltley, Birmingham, and also the much larger Shrewsbury

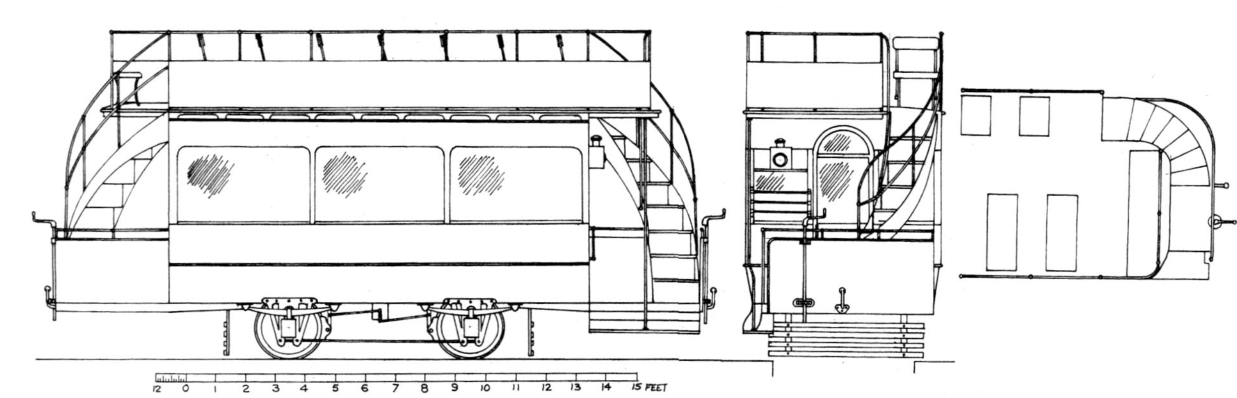

Figure 17: Brown, Marshall, 1895.

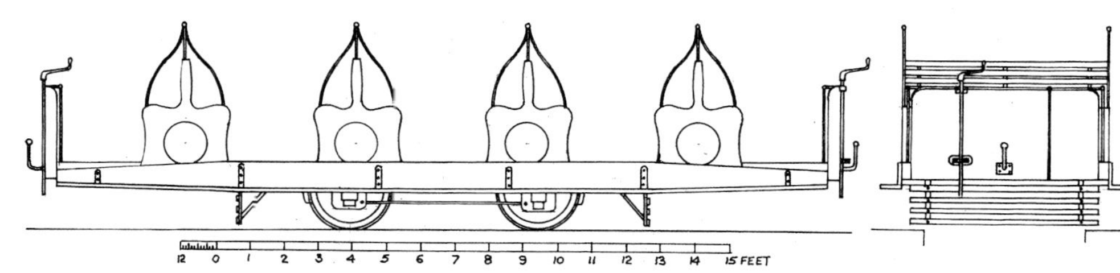

Figure 18: Brown, Marshall, 1878.

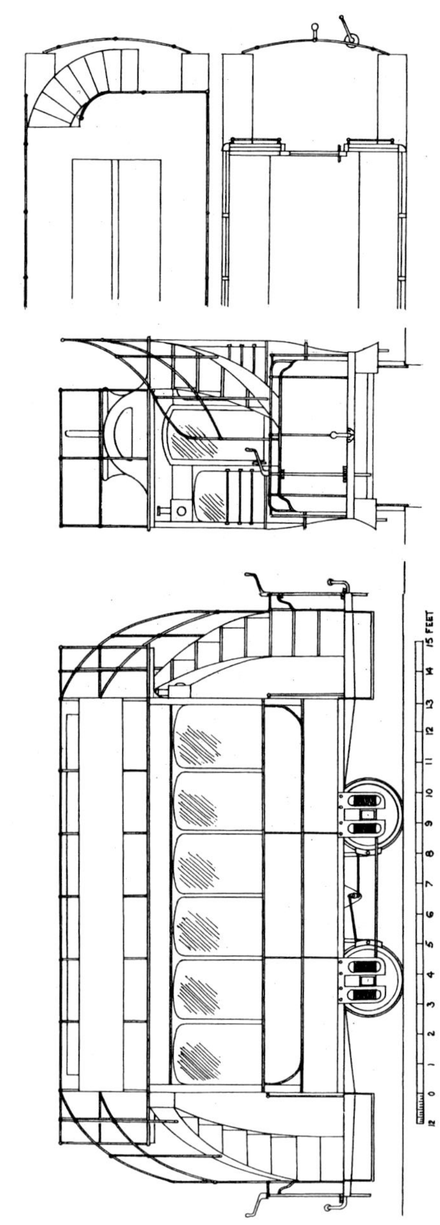

Figure 19: Midland, 1879.

factory built in 1877, were both closed in 1912 and replaced by a new and even-larger building at Washwood Heath that same year. This continues until today to manufacture railway rolling stock, and also became Britain's largest builder of bus bodywork.

Electric Railway & Tramway Carriage Works Ltd, Preston

This company, formed on 25th April, 1898 as a subsidiary of Dick, Kerr & Co. Ltd to take over the building of electric tramcars and railway locomotives, rather strangely began business by constructing 75 horse cars for the London County Council (LCC), and it is thought that this was the only horse car order constructed by this firm. However, after the amalgamation of the company with G.F. Milnes & Co. Ltd, and the British Electric Car Co. Ltd in May 1905, the new company (United Electric Car Co. Ltd) which took over from Electric Railway & Tramway Carriage Works Ltd on 1st July, 1905 did build a handful of horse cars, for Douglas, and the Galway & Salthill Tramways.

It is rather surprising that the LCC should have placed this order for horse cars in 1898, since it was considering converting all its lines to electric working. The design (*Fig. 20*) was to LCC specifications, and therefore cannot be said to have been the maker's own. These cars had low arc roofs and internal clerestory, with reversible 2+2 seats on the upper deck. The seven straight-topped windows had single fixed top lights over them, and one ventilator slot over each window. Stairs were the usual 90° closed tread type, and the platforms had curved dashplates, open on one side only. Entrance to the saloon was by a centrally-placed door with elliptical head, in the top part of which was a vertical slot sliding ventilator. A few years later, a batch of cable cars was built for Edinburgh, but apart from these, the company's whole output was for electric systems.

Manchester Carriage Co. Ltd, Pendleton, Salford

An expansion of Greenwood's five-wheeled bus service, this company constructed most of its own cars in its Salford (Pendleton) workshops, eventually totalling well over 300 vehicles. Its products were very distinctive, featuring a shallow waist panel and an open-sided monitor (*Fig. 21*). John Eades being Works Manager and one of its executives, it is not surprising that some two-thirds of the stock was built on Eades' patent principle, a single-ended car which was reversible on its undercarriage. Actually the reversible car was patented by Stephenson in America in 1855, using practically the same arrangement as Eades. Whether Eades copied Stephenson, or whether he arrived at the same solution independently, cannot be determined, but as Stephenson's patent was an American one, and Eades' an English one, perhaps it was quite legal. This is a point which would need a skilled jurist to unravel.

Cars of the Manchester Carriage Co. pattern were built under licence for other operators by the Ashbury Co., who were also based in Manchester. Reversible seats were fitted on the upper deck – though earlier cars had

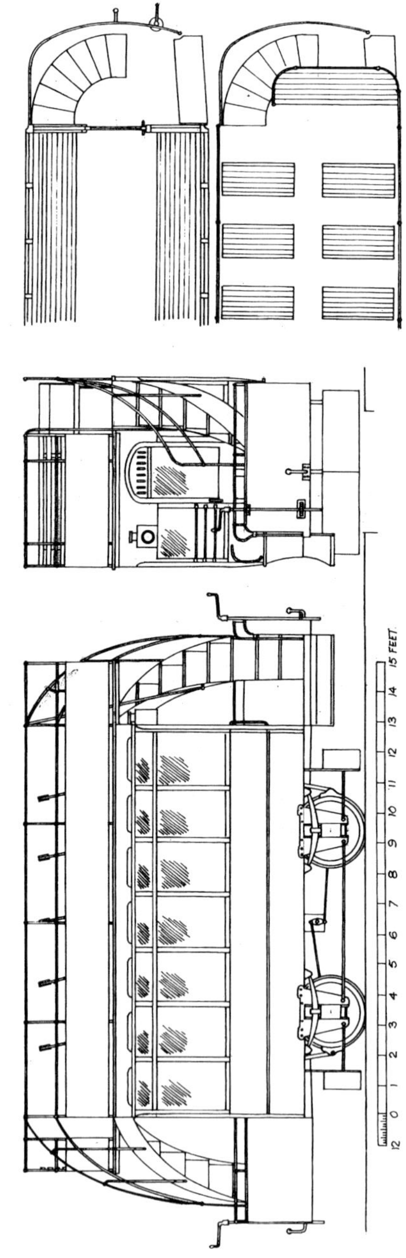

Figure 20: ER&TCW, 1898.

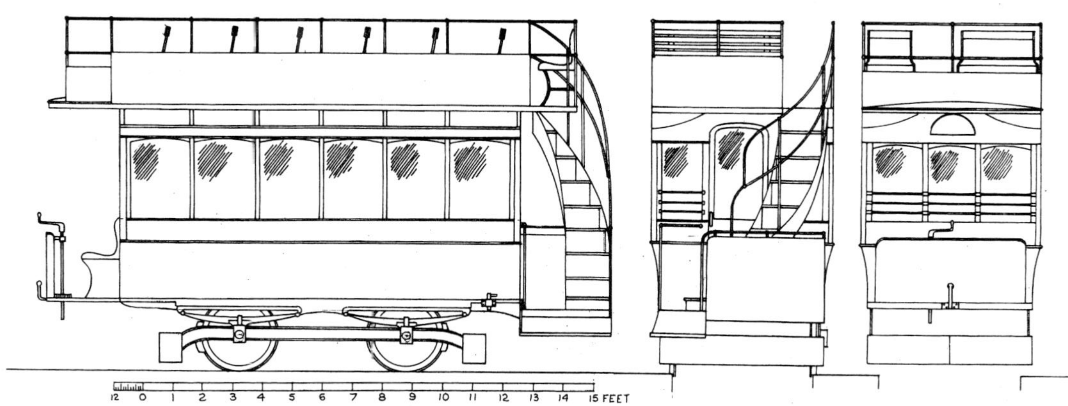

Figure 21: Manchester Carriage Co., 1878.

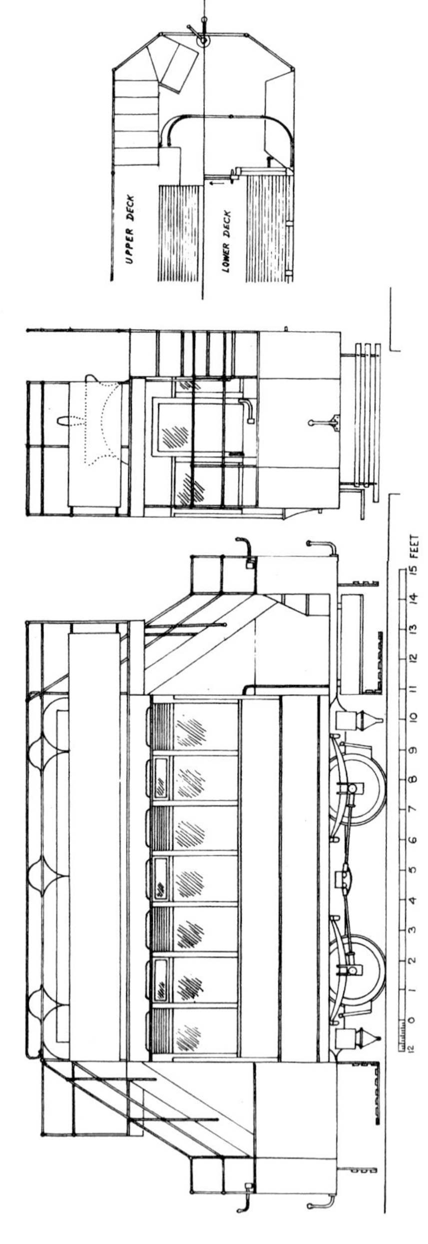

Figure 22: Edinburgh, 1885.

knifeboards – six straight-topped windows were employed, and deep monitor roofs. The saloon door was placed slightly to the left of centre, and had an elliptical head. There was a very short front platform, with a seat for the driver, fixed to the front bulkhead, which had three windows. Dashplates were mostly flat, or only slightly curved, and as the car was reversible, only one set of stairs was required, the seat backs on the top deck being non-reversible.

Eventually, on various dates in 1901, the local authorities of Salford and Manchester bought out the undertaking and electrified it. John Eades had been experimenting on his own account with electric propulsion, converting a horse car in 1898 for this purpose, and when Manchester Corporation was asking for tenders for electric cars, the Carriage Company built one sample car, which became No. 101 in the Manchester fleet, but did not receive any further orders. Pendleton Works remained with the company, and did not build any more trams, horse or electric, and closed after a few years of horse-car repair work.

Other Builders

The Dublin United Tramways Company built 181 horse trams in their own works at Spa Road, Inchicore, during 1882 to 1897. Both the Glasgow and Edinburgh systems built a large number of cars in their own workshops. The Glasgow Corporation Tramways kept strictly to their design, but the Edinburgh Street Tramways Co. varied it slightly, using seven windows instead of six in a number of cars, and replacing alternate top lights with wood slat ventilators. Both companies sold a few of their cars in later years, to other operators in the vicinity, notably to the Greenock & Port Glasgow Tramways, and to the Stirling & Bridge of Allan Co. Edinburgh even purchased 10 cars from Glasgow. One of the Edinburgh cars is shown in *Fig. 22*, though much altered, as it was one of a pair sold to Stirling. The drawing shows it in its final state, as converted to petrol propulsion. The greatest alteration was made to the platforms, which had their round dashplates replaced by angular ones, and the stairs were made straight, except for the bottom two, which came down at an angle of 45° from a small landing. Sandboxes were fitted below the solebars in front of the wheels, and the driving shafts from the central gearbox slung under the frames can be seen. In this form the car was quite successful, and worked for about eight years.

The set-up at Edinburgh is worthy of note, as it was somewhat complicated. The Edinburgh Street Tramways Co. (EST) operated from 1871, and was entirely a horse-operated company, with a network of 18½ route miles. Meanwhile, the Edinburgh Northern Tramways Company commenced two cable-worked lines in 1888 and 1890. Five years later, it was decided to convert all the Edinburgh tramways to cable working, but the separate Burgh of Leith (which had horse lines worked by the EST) did not want cable cars. Faced with this problem, the EST decided to form a separate company, Edinburgh & District Tramways Co. Ltd (E&DT) to take over the cable working, leaving the original company to work the horse lines in Leith. To this end, they made over 70 of their horse cars in 1897 to the new company, which subsequently

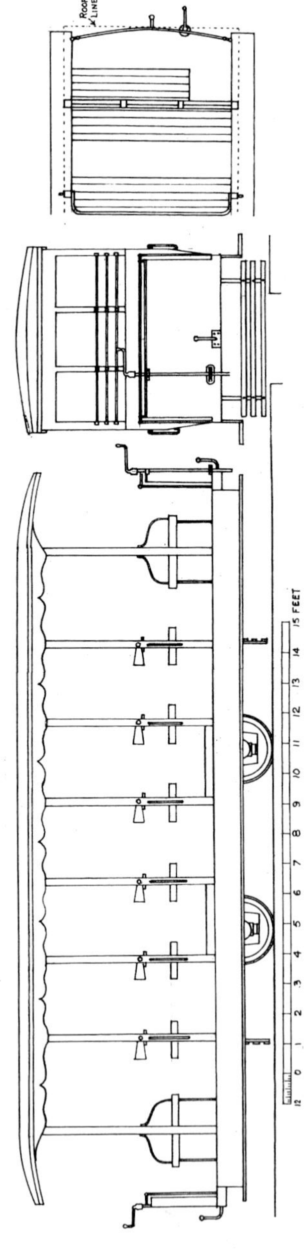

Figure 23: Milnes, Voss & Co., 1911.

converted many of them for cable working, and retained 30 to work the lines in Leith. In 1904, Leith Corporation took over the lines within the Burgh, and for nearly a year operated the horse cars themselves, until the electrification was completed. The cable cars of the E&DT continued to work until 1919, when they were taken over by Edinburgh Corporation and gradually electrified over the next three years. Actually, the last horse-operated route in the district was that to Colinton, which was not converted until 1907.

Glasgow Corporation replaced the Glasgow Tramways & Omnibus Co. in 1894, and operated horse cars to its standard design until 1902. There were a number of different firms who built odd horse cars from time to time, some fairly well known, but others obscure, and not heard of outside their own particular area. In this category came Shinnie (Aberdeen), Swinton (Dundee), Croall (Edinburgh), Drew & Burnett (Edinburgh), Boyall (Grantham), East End Foundry (Sheffield), Malcolm's Boatyard (Port Bannatyne), and William Lauder & Co. (Rothesay). The last three built six, four, and five cars respectively for the Rothesay Tramways Co. A company known as the Tramway Car & Works Co., with headquarters at Greenwich and a branch works in Glasgow, flourished for rather less than 10 years, building cars for the London companies, and for Glasgow, though it found little work elsewhere, during the 1870s.

Few horse cars were built after 1900, as the existing systems were getting fewer and fewer, until by 1926 only one was left, Douglas Corporation. Thus when Douglas required some new cars, they had difficulty in finding builders. The first orders for replacements, between 1905 and 1913, were placed with G.C. Milnes, Voss & Co., of Birkenhead, which supplied six cars during this period. They differed in seating capacity, and in the profile of the roof and cant rail boards. One of the 1911 cars is shown by *Fig. 23*. G.C. Milnes was the son of George F. Milnes, and after the failure of his father's company, set up a works in Cleveland Street, Birkenhead (but *not* the original Milnes building) and took into partnership his father's chief draughtsman Thomas Voss. Between 1906 and 1914, when the firm closed down, G.C. Milnes, Voss & Co. produced very few complete cars, its main output being in the form of top-covers for the conversion of open-top electric cars. The six horse cars built for Douglas were the only ones ever built by this firm.

The North Metropolitan Tramways Co. also began building horse cars for its own system, and a few were sold to other companies including Portsmouth, Southampton, Plymouth and Dublin. It set up a works for this purpose in Union Road, Leytonstone, in 1884. The United Electric Car Co. of Preston also built two 40-seater toast racks for Douglas in 1907, and five double-deck cars for the Galway & Salthill Tramway (Ireland) about the same time. Two railway companies built horse cars for their own use, the Caledonian Railway in 1887 for its Inchture Tramway (previous to this date an ordinary four-wheeled railway coach was used), and the South Eastern & Chatham Railway is said to have built two or three cars for the Hythe line. The Great Northern Railway of Ireland owned one double-deck car built by the Metropolitan Railway Carriage & Wagon Co. in 1883 for the Fintona Tramway.

Milnes, Voss having gone out of business, the very last horse trams to be built in this country were constructed in 1935 (until the construction of the Bradford

The North Metropolitan Tramways Co. owned and operated a very dense network of horse tramway routes in the north-eastern quarter of what became the County of London, from the Holborn to Highgate area out to the Essex county boundary at the River Lea, and also a few in West Ham and Leyton. This grew gradually from 1870 up to a maximum of 56¼ route miles with 668 cars. But most of this (48½ miles) was compulsorily purchased by the London County Council on 27th May, 1897, although it continued to be operated on a lease until 1st April, 1906. The LCC then took over operation as well, electrifying the routes only gradually, and the last horse car did not run until 1914. This photograph shows a typical North Metropolitan knifeboard seat car at Clapton in 1879 on the route from there to Moorgate. The company built most of its own trams itself, at Unwin Road, Leytonstone.   *Topical Press*

This car, which was probably built by the North Metropolitan Tramways Co. in its own factory at Union Road, Leytonstone, is seen standing at the northern end of Liverpool Road, the terminus of the short one mile route from Holloway Road to Upper Street, Islington. It has been repainted in London County Council livery after the company was compulscrily taken over by the LCC on 1st April, 1906. Most of the other North Metropolitan routes were electrified in the next few years, but this Liverpool Road route was not, and it survived with horse cars until abandoned on 19th July, 1913 without any replacement. This photograph would date from 1907 to 1913.

The South Eastern Metropolitan Tramways Co. owned and operated one solitary route, 2½ miles long, from London Street, Greenwich, via South Street, Lewisham Road and Lewisham High Street, to Rushey Green, Catford. This was a late starter, not opening until 11th October, 1890. There were eventually 12 cars, all built by the North Metropolitan company at Union Road, Leytonstone, to its standard 46-seat garden-seat design. This photograph shows the first car, actually at the Union Road Works when brand new. *Tramway & Railway World*

tramcar depicted on the front cover) by a motor-bus and lorry works, the Vulcan Motor & Engineering Co. Ltd, of Southport, Lancashire for Douglas Corporation. The Vulcan had had some experience of building toast-rack bodies, which it fitted to motor chassis of its own manufacture for service in seaside resorts. These three, Douglas Nos. 48-50, were roofed toast racks with 34 seats, seven benches for four, and a seat for three on each platform. They were designed as all-weather cars, having a system of folding side screens, and the end seat of each bench made to fold up, leaving a side gangway. In this form, the cars seated 27. Most Douglas cars were fitted with new trunnions and roller-bearing axle boxes designed and made by Maley & Taunton Ltd, of Wednesbury, Staffordshire between 1934 and 1955.

So the horse tram lives on, not dead, and far from moribund, but to take a look at it, and sample its almost silent, leisurely progress along its track, the traveller must take a journey to the Isle of Man, and along the shore of Douglas Bay he can imagine himself back in the days of a century ago when the horse tram was a novelty. In these days of sophisticated diesel and electric transport, the horse-drawn public vehicle is again a novelty - the wheel has come full circle. Let it be hoped that Douglas Corporation does not succumb to the wiles of those (and there are some) who would have the horse trams abolished, and that their undoubted tourist attraction will remain for many years to come.

A peaceful scene in Dalston Lane in around 1903, as a North Metropolitan garden-seated horse car on a route completed on 5th August, 1879, almost the last of the huge North Metropolitan network, is seen passing Dalston Junction station on the North London Railway, which had opened on 1st November, 1865. The rear of a typical horse omnibus can be seen on the left.   *Charles Martin*

Here is one of the seven horse trams owned and operated by the Exeter Tramways Co. Ltd on the three very short routes totalliing only 2¼ miles, from 6th April, 1882 until 4th April, 1905. The Exeter Corporation took over in 1904 and electrified and extended the routes in 1905.

List of Horse Tramways in the British Isles

Dates shown are those of horse-working, not incorporation.

	Dates	No. of Cars	Mileage
Aberdeen District Tramways Co.* (*ff*)	1874-1902	50	10 ½
Aldershot & Farnborough Light Railway Co.* (*a*)	1881-1883	2	2 ½
Belfast Street Tramways Co.*	1872-1905	144	25 ¼
Birkdale & Southport Tramways Co.*	1883-1902	6	4
Birkenhead Street Railway Co. Ltd (*b*)	1860-1889	8	4
Birkenhead United Tramways & Carriage Co. Ltd (*b*)	1889-1901	27	10 ¾
Birmingham Central Tramways Co. Ltd (*hh*)	1886-1896	126	25
Birmingham & District Tramways Co. Ltd	1872-1876	22	8
Birmingham & Midland Tramways Co. Ltd (*d*)	1883-1901	2	1 ½
Birmingham Tramways & Omnibus Co. Ltd (*hh*)	1876-1885	66	11 ½
Blackburn Corporation Tramways Co. Ltd	1888-1899	8	3 ¾
Blackpool, St Annes & Lytham Tramways Co. (*bb*)	1900-1901	22	5 ½
Blackrock & Kingstown Tramways Co.* (Dublin)	1885-1896	6	2 ½
Bolton Corporation Tramways (*c*)	1880-1899	48	19
Bradford Tramways & Omnibus Co. Ltd	1882-1902	18	2 ½
Brighton & Shoreham Tramways Co. Ltd	1884-1913	11	4 ½
Bristol Tramways & Carriage Co. Ltd	1875-1900	109	9 ½
Cardiff Tramways Co. Ltd	1872-1902	52	6 ⅓
Cardiff District & Penarth Harbour Tr. Co. Ltd	1881-1903	11	2 ½
Cambridge Street Tramways Co.*	1880-1914	8	2 ¾
Chester Tramways Co.*	1879-1902	11	2 ½
Chesterfield & District Tramways Co. Ltd	1882-1904	8	1 ¼
City of Birmingham Tramways Co. Ltd (*hh*)	1896-1906	161	16 ½
City of Derry Tramways Co.*	1897-1919	7	1 ½
City of Gloucester Tramways Co. Ltd	1879-1902	14	3 ¼
City of Oxford & District Tramways Co. Ltd	1882-1913	19	6 ¼
City of York Tramways Co.	1886-1909	10	2 ¾
Cork Tramways Co. Ltd	1872-1875	6	2
Croydon Tramways Co.* (*aa*)	1879-1901	18	5
Derby Tramways Co. Ltd	1880-1900	16	4 ¾
Dewsbury, Batley & Birstal Tramways Co.* (*oo*)	1874-1881	7	4 ¼
Darlington & Stockton Steam Tramways Co. Ltd (*ee*)	1880-1903	7	2
Darlington Street Railroad Co. (G.F. Train)	1862-1865	4	2
Douglas Corporation (*g*)	1902-	50	2 ¼
Dublin Central Tramways Co.*	1879-1881	30	6 ½
Dublin Tramways Co.*	1872-1881	82	16 ½
Dublin United Tramways Co. Ltd	1881-1901	186	35 ¼
Dublin Southern District Tramways Co.*	1879-1896	26	6 ¼
Dundee & District Tramways Co.*	1877-1901	24	7 ¼
Dudley, Sedgley & Wolverhampton Tr. Co. Ltd (*f*)	1883-1885	7	5 ¾
East Anglian Tramway Co.* (Yarmouth)	1875-1878	10	2 ¾
Edinburgh Street Tramways Co.* (*h*)	1871-1894	84	18 ½
Edinburgh & District Tramways Co. Ltd	1894-1907	30	25 ½
Exeter Tramways Company Ltd	1882-1903	5	2 ¼

The City of Gloucester Tramways Co. Ltd had a small horse tramway system of only 3⅔ miles, comprising five very short sections radiating from The Cross, all opening on 24th May, 1879. There were six cars at the opening, later 10, and then 13, a mixed bag some built by Bristol Wagon Co., some by a predecessor of Brush, and some by the local Gloucester Railway Carriage & Wagon Co. Ltd, all being small four-wheelers. Here in about 1900 we see one of them, at the Southgate Street terminus, usually known as the Royal Infirmary. It is reversing, and we can see the driver and conductor and the horse, walking around the car and carrying the coupling traces to the other end. The trams in the left and right distance are respectively going to and coming from the Bristol Road terminus at Theresa Place, half a mile further on.

Pamlin Prints

	Dates	No. of Cars	Mileage
Fairbourne Tramway (*j*)	1890-1916	2	1 ¾
Fintona Tramway	1854-1957	1	¾
Folkestone, Sandgate & Hythe Tramway Co.* (*k*)	1891-1921	5	3 ⅓
Galway & Salthill Tramway Co.*	1878-1919	7	2 ¼
Glasgow Tramway & Omnibus Co. Ltd (*l*)	1872-1894	233	31 ½
Glasgow Corporation	1894-1902	385	35
Glasgow & Ibrox Tramway Co.* (*m*)	1879-1891	4	1 ½
Glenanne & Loughgilly Tramway	1897-1919	1	2 ½
Glyn Valley Tramway* (*f*)	1873-1888	4	7 ½
Gravesend, Rosherville & Northfleet Tr. Co. Ltd	1883-1901	6	2 ¼
Great Grimsby Street Tramways Co.*	1881-1901	16	5 ½
Greenock & Port Glasgow Tramways Co.* (*jj*)	1889-1901	21	7 ½
Harrow Road & Paddington Tramway Co.*	1888-1906	22	2 ¾
Hoylake & Birkenhead Rail & Tramway Co.* (*b*)	1873-1901	8	2 ¼
Huddersfield Corporation (*cc*)	1885-1888	2	1 ½
Hull Street Tramways Co. Ltd	1873-1901	39	8 ¾
Inchture Tramway (Caledonian Railway) (*gg*)	1849-1916	1	1 ½
Ipswich Tramways Co.*	1880-1903	9	4 ¼
Isle of Man Tramways Ltd (*g*)	1876-1902	37	1 ¾
Keighley Tramways Co. Ltd	1888-1904	7	2 ¼
Lancaster & District Tramways Co.*	1890-1921	14	4 ¼
Landport & Southsea Tramways Co.* (*o*)	1865-1883	(?) 8	2 ¼
Lea Bridge, Leyton & Walthamstow Tr. Co.* (*z*)	1883-1906	22	4 ¾
Leamington & Warwick Tramways & Omnibus Co. Ltd	1881-1905	7	3
Leeds Tramways Co.*	1871-1901	77	17
Leicester Tramways Co.*	1874-1904	46	8 ¾
Lincoln Tramway Co. Ltd	1882-1905	11	1 ¾
Liverpool Tramways Co.*	1869-1876	16	7
Liverpool United Tramways & Omnibus Co. Ltd	1876-1903	281	42 ¾
Llanelly Tramways Co. Ltd (*n*)	1882-1911	5	6 ¼
London, Camberwell & Dulwich Tr. Co.* (*x*)	1896-1900	6	3
London County Council - Northern Area (*nn*)	1896-1914	0	50 ½
London County Council - Southern Area (*nn*)	1899-1915	517	53 ½
London, Deptford & Greenwich Tr. Co.*	1880-1904	42	5
London Street Tramways Co.*	1871-1897	136	13 ½
London Southern Tramways Co.*	1884-1906	32	5 ¾
London Tramways Co. Ltd (*y*)	1874-1898	435	24 ¼
Manchester Carriage & Tramways Co.*	1877-1903	519	87
Marble Arch Street Rail Co. Ltd (*p*)	1861-1862	2	1 ½
Metropolitan Street Tramways Co.*	1870-1874	?	6
Middlesbrough & Stockton Tramways Co.*	1874-1897	12	2 ½
Morecambe Tramways Co.*	1887-1926	17	4
Neath & District Tramways Co.* (*w*)	1875-1899	11	4
Newcastle & Gosforth Tramways & Carriage Co. Ltd	1878-1899	44	11 ½
Newport Corporation (Mon.)	1894-1903	26	5
Newport Tramways Co.* (Mon.)	1875-1894	8	1 ½
Northampton Street Tramways Co.*	1880-1904	25	5 ¼
North Dublin Street Tramways Co.*	1876-1881	25	8
North London Tramways Co.* (*r*)	1881-1891	25	8 ½
North Metropolitan Tramways Co.* (*pp*)	1870-1906	668	56 ¼
Nottingham & District Tramways Co. Ltd	1878-1897	38	10 ½

The Lea Bridge, Leyton & Walthamstow Tramways Co. owned and operated horse tramways along Lea Bridge Road and Woodford New Road from Cornthwaite Road, Clapton, as far as the Rising Sun Inn opposite the end of Upper Walthamstow Road, with a branch from the Bakers Arms Inn along Leyton High Street and High Road almost to Leyton station on the Great Eastern Railway. This picture, which shows the first part of the line to be opened, on 12th May, 1883, is in Lea Bridge Road looking towards Woodford, with the High Street branch at the bottom right, and the Bakers Arms Inn and Hoe Street just off the bottom left. The company eventually owned 22 horse trams, but it was taken over in 1905 by Leyton Urban District Council, who electrified the routes in 1906.

The London Tramways Co. Ltd had horse tramways which ran from the south sides of Westminster and Blackfriars bridges via Kennington to Brixton, ending at Water Lane at the foot of Brixton Hill. To extend southwards up the hill it was felt that something better than horse traction was needed. So the Brixton Road tramway from Kennington (Church Row, now Prima Road) to Water Lane was converted to cable operation, and a new cable tramway was built from here to Telford Avenue, Streatham. Both were opened to traffic on 19th December, 1892, a total of 2¾ miles. A moving endless cable in a slot under the road surface, pulled from a power station at Telford Avenue, was gripped or released as required, by a gripper underneath a separate tractor or dummy, which pulled a standard double-deck passenger horse car, to which it was coupled or uncoupled at Church Row, the latter then being pulled by horses from or to the Bridges to give a through service. In 1899 enough passenger cars were fitted with cable grippers, and separate tractors ceased to be used. But the through service thus ceased and passengers had to change cars at Church Row. This photograph shows a car on the Streatham to Blackfriars service after it had been taken over by the LCC on 1st January, 1899. The cable route was later closed on 5th April, 1904 for the normal electrification.

	Dates	No. of Cars	Mileage
Nottingham Corporation	1898-1901	38	10 ½
Oldham Corporation (*dd*)	1880-1901	0	5
Paisley Tramways Co. Ltd	1886-1903	8	2 ½
Perth & District Tramways Co. Ltd	1895-1905	9	4 ¼
Pimlico, Peckham & Greenwich Street Tramways Co.*	1871-1874	?	10
Pontypridd & Rhondda Valley Tramway Co.*	1888-1903	14	3
Plymouth, Stonehouse & Devonport Tramway Co.	1872-1901	27	2
Plymouth Corporation	1893-1907	26	5 ¼
Portsmouth Street Tramways Co.*	1874-1903	65	14
Preston Tramways Co.* (*s*)	1879-1886	6	2 ½
Preston Corporation (*mm*)	1882-1903	25	4 ½
Pwllheli & Llanbedrog (S. Andrews & Son Ltd)	1896-1927	(?) 21	3 ¾
Pwllheli Corporation	1899-1920	3	½
Reading Tramways Co.*	1879-1903	13	2 ½
Rothesay Tramways Co. Ltd	1882-1902	19	2 ½
Ryde Pier Company's Tramway (*t*)	1864-1886	3	1 ¼
St Helens & District Tramways Co.* (*f*)	1881-1899	12	9
Sheffield Tramways Co.* (*u*)	1873-1896	53	9 ¼
Sheffield Corporation	1896-1902	53	9 ¼
South Eastern Metropolitan Tramways Co.*	1890-1902	12	2 ½
South London Tramways Co.*	1881-1902	85	12 ¾
Southampton Tramways Co.*	1879-1900	40	4 ¾
Southport Tramways Co. Ltd	1873-1901	13	6 ¼
South Shields Tramways & Carriage Co. Ltd (*v*)	1883-1906	25	2 ¾
Staffordshire Potteries Street Railway Co. Ltd (*e*)	1862-1882	5	1 ½
Stirling & Bridge of Allan Tramway Co. Ltd	1874-1920	17	3 ½
Stockport & Hazel Grove Carriage & Tr. Co. Ltd	1888-1904	14	3 ½
Stockton & Darlington Steam Tramways Co. Ltd (*ee*)	1881-1903	7	3 ¼
Sunderland Tramways Co.*	1879-1900	32	8 ½
Surrey Side Street Rail Co. Ltd (*p*)	1861-1862	2	1
Swansea Improvements & Tramways Co. Ltd	1878-1900	25	5 ½
Tynemouth & District Tramways Ltd	1881-1883	3	2 ½
Vale of Clyde Tramways Co.*	1872-1894	26	6 ¾
Wallasey United Tramway & Omnibus Co. Ltd	1879-1901	14	3 ¼
Warrenpoint & Rostrevor Tramway Co.*	1877-1915	13	3 ¼
West Metropolitan Tramways Co.* (*qq*)	1874-1901	58	8 ¾
Westminster Street Rail Co. Ltd (*p*)	1861-1862	2	½
Wigan Tramways Co. Ltd (*kk*)	1880-1885	12	7 ¾
Wirral Tramway Co. Ltd (*b*)	1877-1901	20	3
Woolwich & South East London Tramways Co. Ltd	1881-1905	33	5
Wolverhampton Tramways Co. Ltd	1878-1901	25	9 ¼
Worcester Tramways Ltd	1882-1903	10	3 ¼
Wrexham District Tramways Co.*	1876-1901	3	3 ¼
Yarmouth & Gorleston Tramways Co. Ltd	1878-1905	10	2 ¾
York Tramways Co. Ltd	1880-1886	10	2 ¾

Notes

(*a*) Operated intermittently, continued, not continuous, for short periods approximately 1888 to 1898.

(*b*) Birkenhead Street Railway Co. Ltd was taken over by Birkenhead Tramways Co. 1877 then by Birkenhead Corporation 1889 (leased to Birkenhead United Tramways, Omnibus & Carriage Co. Ltd). The Hoylake & Birkenhead Rail & Tramway Co. taken over by Birkenhead Tramways Co. 1879, then taken over by Birkenhead Corporation 1889 (leased to Birkenhead United Tramways, Omnibus & Carriage Co. Ltd). Wirral Tramway Co. was leased from Birkenhead Corporation 1895. Temporary replacement service operated by Birkenhead United Tramways, Omnibus & Carriage Co. Ltd 1900-1901, during electrification.

(*c*) Leased to E. Holden & Co.

(*d*) Leased to J. Crowther. This was only a very small part of the B&MT system, which was mostly steam.

(*e*) Replaced in 1882 by steam tramway of another company.

(*f*) No passenger service 1886-1888, then steam with another company 1889-1899.

(*g*) Taken over by Douglas Corporation from Isle of Man Tramways Co. in 1902.

(*h*) EST retained 5 miles of lines in Leith until 1904 (operated by Leith Corporation 1904-1905). Remainder transferred to E&DT Co. in 1894.

(*j*) Laid for brickworks, passengers in season; gauge reduced from 2 ft to 15 in. in 1916 and converted to miniature steam railway, and still exists as such.

(*k*) Purchased and operated by South Eastern Railway from 1893.

(*l*) Replaced by Glasgow Corporation 1894 without purchase or transfer.

(*m*) Purchased by Burgh of Govan 1891, and leased to Glasgow Tramways & Omnibus Co.

(*n*) Purchased by Llanelly Corporation and electrified 1911.

(*o*) Taken over by Portsmouth Street Tramways Co. 1883.

(*p*) G.F. Train's tramways - never LCC property.

(*r*) Worked by horse 1881-1885, then steam-operated 1885-1891, then horse again 1891-1892. Sold to North Metropolitan Tramways Co. 1892.

(*s*) Worked by horse 1881-1185, then sold to Preston Corporation 1886, but company lines leased to Harding & Co. Ltd 1887 to 1903. (Corporation figures include company cars and mileage.)

(*t*) Originally Pierhead to St John's Road 1864-1880 (jointly owned by the LBSCR and LSWR). Then Pierhead to Esplanade 1880-1886 owned by Pier Tramway Co. Railway, and operated by steam 1881-1884, and after 1886 electric and later petrol, subsequently purchased by the Southern Railway.

(*u*) Taken over by Sheffield Corporation 1896.

(*v*) Company failed 1886. Reconstituted and re-opened 1887.

(*w*) Purchased by Neath Corporation in 1897 and worked with gas-engined cars from 1899.

(*x*) Constructed 1885, but prevented from working until 1895, through disputes with local authorities.

(*y*) Formed in 1874 by amalgamation of Metropolitan Street Tramways Co. and Pimlico, Peckham & Greenwich Street Tramways Co., both of which had opened in 1870.

(*z*) Went into liquidation 1885 and closed. Re-formed under same title and re-opened 1889. Purchased by Leyton UDC 1905, electrified 1906.

(*aa*) Two of the five routes were opened in 1883 by a separate Norwood & District Tramways Co. The two companies soon amalgamated as the Croydon & Norwood Tramways Co., and this was taken over in 1889 by a new Croydon Tramways Co.

(*bb*) Operated by British Gas Traction Co. Ltd 1896-1903. The horse trams were second-hand, purely temporary, to cover mechanical trouble with gas cars.

(*cc*) Only Moldgreen route, all others steam.

(*dd*) Leased to Manchester Carriage & Tramways Co.

(*ee*) Purchased by Imperial Tramways Co. Ltd 1896, mainly steam 1881-1898, but horse-worked to 1903.

(*ff*) Operated by Aberdeen Corporation 1898-1902.

(*gg*) Worked by one railway coach 1849 to 1895. Tramcar not until 1895.

(*hh*) The statistics for mileage and numbers of cars include mostly steam and cable tramways. Only a small part was horse, exact figures not known.

(*jj*) Including portions leased from Greenock Corporation and from Gourock Corporation.

(*kk*) Some of this 7¾ was steam. All routes steam after 1885.

(*mm*) Always operated by W. Harding & Co. Ltd.

(*nn*) Southern half owned and operated by LCC. Northern half owned by LCC and operated by North Metropolitan on a lease.

(*oo*) Worked with steam 1880 to 1905.

(*pp*) Most of it was acquired by LCC, but not all. Some parts went to West Ham Corporation and to the Metropolitan Electric Tramways.

(*qq*) Sold to London United Tramways Ltd in 1894.

* Statutory companies, not limited.

Bibliography

Light Railway Transport League Publications - now the Light Rail Transit Association:
Modern Tramway
Tramway Review
Tramways of East Anglia (Anderson)
Tramways of Portsmouth (Harrison)
The Tramways of Birkenhead & Wallasey (T.B. Maund & M. Jenkins)

Scottish Tramway Museum Society - now the Scottish Tramway & Transport Society:
Tramways of Greenock & Port Glasgow (Cormack)
Tramways of the Tay Valley (Brotchie)
Tramways of Stirling (Brotchie)
The Glasgow Horse Tramways, S.J.T. Robertson, Scottish Tramway & Transport Society

North British Traction Society:
Scottish Tramway Fleets (Brotchie)

The Oakwood Press:
Lancaster & Morecambe Tramways (Shuttleworth)
Cambridge Street Tramways (Swingle)

Turntable Publications:
Edinburgh Tramways Album (Hunter)
Hundred Years of Leeds Tramways (Young)

Other Publishers:
The British Tram (Wilson), Percival Marshall
Horse Cars, Cable Cars & Omnibuses (White), Dover Publications, New York
Dick Kerr Album (Hyde & Pearson), pub. Authors
Black Country Tramways (Webb), pub. Author
St Helens Tramways (Stretch), pub. Author
Tramways or Northumberland (Hearse), pub. Author
Tramways of South Shields (Hearse), pub. Author
Isle of Man Tramways (Pearson), David & Charles
Tramways of Salford (Gray), Manchester Transport Museum Soc.
Irish Trams (James Kilroy), Colourpoint
Through Streets Broad and Narrow, A History of Dublin Trams (Michael Corcoran), Midland Publishing
The Douglas Horse Tramway (Keith Pearson), Adam Gordon
Manchester Carriage and Tramways Company (Edward Gray), Manchester Transport Museum Soc.
History of the J.G. Brill Company (Debra Brill), Indiana University Press
British Tramway Guide, 4th Edition (Paul H. Abell), AB Publishing

This list is not exhaustive; it includes those consulted by the author.